ORDO CALENDAR

of the

ANGLICAN RITE ROMAN CATHOLIC CHURCH

2021 – 2022

BY

COURT OF ST. MARY OF WALSINGHAM

D1506579

THE ANGLICAN PATRIARCHATE
(SEE OF ST. STEPHEN)

STATO PONTIFICIO

ORDO CALENDAR

of the

ANGLICAN RITE ROMAN CATHOLIC CHURCH

2021 – 2022

by

Court of St. Mary of Walsingham

LITURGICAL YEAR OF
POPE SAINT PIUS IX

RVTHERFORDVS PP. I PONT. MAGNVS

THE ANGLICAN PATRIARCHATE OF ROME

(OLD ROMAN CATHOLIC OF THE ANGLICAN RITE)

St. George Seminary Press

St. George Seminary Press

www.anglicancommonprayer.org/

First published in this Edition: 2021

Imprimi Potest: ✠Em.mus ac Rev.mus Keith *Card.* Steinhurst
Electorus Archiepiscopus titularis Treviae
06 September 2021

Printed and Bound in the United States of America.
21 20 10 9 8 7 6 5 4 3 2 1

Introduction

TO THE 2021-2022 Ordo Calendar

❧❧

The Ordo Calendar assumes familiarity with the rubrics of both the missal and the breviary. For each day is provided the main liturgical event for the day, whether it be a feast, an octave, a feria, or a vigil. Underneath are provided the required commemorations for that day in order of rank. The listings for each day are also used to determine which Offices to recite from the breviary and which commemorations to make at Vespers and Lauds. Note, however, that the commemorations given in this Ordo for the mass may not always be made in the Offices, according to the rubrics provided in the breviary. Other exceptions are noted in this Ordo.

LIMITATION OF NUMBER OF MASSES
CELEBRATED BY ONE PRIEST IN A DAY

A priest may typically only celebrate one mass in a day. Where permitted in rubrics, this is dispensed. Also, in parishes of limited clergy, this may be dispensed as well by episcopal authority. In no case shall a priest celebrate more than three masses in a day. Priests celebrating more than one mass in a day should follow the procedures given for All Souls Day in terms of purification of the Sacred Vessels.

RANKS OF VOTIVE MASSES

Votive masses are assumed to have the rank of fourth class, unless otherwise noted. That is, except where noted, they may only be said as the principal mass on days that are either ferial or of a simple feast. The exceptions are the Requiem mass and the Nuptial mass, which are discussed above.

Certain votive masses may be given "permanent" rank, either always or only under certain circumstances or at certain times. Rank may go from 4th class to 1st class. Additionally, votive masses may be given "particular" rank, that is, rank that applies not universally, but only in certain congregations or dioceses. For example, the votive mass(es) pertaining to the patron saint of a parish may be given special rank so that they may be said on a Sunday. Promotion of votive masses is done only under episcopal authority.

Additionally, certain votive masses may be given higher rank for special occasions and circumstances. These situations typically entail the votive mass said with higher rank on a single occasion. For example, this may be done during time of great need, or to give thanksgiving.

COLORS FOR VOTIVE MASSES

There are no fixed colors for votive masses. On any day the color of the day is purple, 4th class votive masses should be said wearing purple (or rose, if during a "rose week"). If votive masses are said as above for a special occasion with higher rank, a specific color may be specified. Otherwise, general color customs are as below:

Votives Masses of Our Lord:	White
Of Our Lady:	White or Marian Blue
Of the Holy Spirit and the Passion:	Red
Of the Sick or for any Type of Tribulation or Petition:	Purple

If the votive mass is of a Saint or some other feast given in the missal, then the color is the same as on the feast. Otherwise, the choice of the color is up to the priest, with the caveat that the symbolism of the color choice should make sense, both to the mass and to the situation and circumstances under which it is being said.

NOTES ON PRAYING THE OFFICES IN THE ANGLO-ROMAN BREVIARY 2021

Rutherford Pp. I

General Notes

The general rubrics may be found in the front of the breviary. These notes are designed to provide further explanation, as well as to give general historical context and various optional uses. The offices may be said or sung either in public or in private. The various postures given assume a traditional public liturgy. They are often modified as necessary in private recitations.

The great offices, or the major offices, are Matins, Lauds, and Vespers. Matins and Lauds are traditionally joined together and essentially comprise one office, though they may be separated as appropriate, particularly in private recitations. The little hours, or the minor offices, are the remaining five. Matins and Lauds are traditionally said in the morning – particularly in the early morning. Before they were joined together, Matins was typically said at midnight, and Lauds at around three in the morning. The offices from Prime through Compline, then, mark the waking hours throughout the day and used to be used as a means of telling time. The offices need not be said at exactly the time specified, but it is good to be in at least the same general region of the day. Whenever they are recited, they should go in order.

Clerics, as well as religious brothers and sisters, typically sit in choir and sing or recite the offices. There is a cantor, who intones the antiphons and begins the Psalms, a lector who reads or sings the lessons, and an officiant, often referred to as the "foremost," who begins the offices, sings the collects, leads the versicles and responses, and leads the preces.

The standard vesture for clerics and religious brothers and sisters, particularly in public offices, is choir dress. Clerics wear the zucchetto. At Solemn Matins, Lauds, and Vespers, the officiating cleric or religious brother wears an alb, rope cincture, and cope in the colour of the day, along with a biretta and zucchetto. Those directly assisting the officiant vest similarly. The biretta as usual is only worn while processing by the foremost. All others carry it while processing and wear it only while sitting. (A greater prelate, however, who is officiating, but not acting as the foremost, still wears the biretta while processing. A Cardinal always wears it in procession.)

A bishop or other entitled to the cappa magna wears it at solemn Matins, with the hood over the head, and solemnly vests into the cope in the usual manner during the Psalms of Lauds. Similarly, a Bishop or other entitled to the cappa magna at solemn vespers wears it to begin the office, but changes during the Psalms into the cope. A bishop in cappa magna therefore does not wear a biretta. Stoles are not worn during the offices except by foremost if a priest, and then only during solemn Matins, Lauds, and Vespers when wearing the cope.

Notes on the Sunday Offices

The Sunday offices are said of the Sunday unless the feast appointed for Sunday is the first or second class. This applies even if there is a feast of double or greater double rank that would be appointed in place of a specific regular semi-double Sunday.

Some Sundays have first or second class rank, but are specified in the liturgical calendar to be said as if they were a semi-double in the offices. This is denoted in the calendar as, for example, "s2, sd., p." for a Sunday of the Second Class, with liturgical colour of purple, that is to be said as if it were a semi-double. That means that the preces will still be said, despite the rank of the Sunday, and the antiphons are not doubled. (And this occurs on certain feasts as well.)

Since the Sunday goes from Matins to Compline, all offices through Compline on Saturday are simply of whatever feast or feria is appointed for that Saturday.

At Vespers on Sunday, it is typically of the Sunday. If there is a feast to commemorate occurring on that Sunday, it is generally commemorated. However, since feasts of saints go from Vespers to Vespers and thus span two days, there is the possibility of a I Vespers on Sunday for a feast on the following Monday. If there is no appointed commemoration for II Vespers of a feast on Sunday, then the I Vespers of the Monday feast is commemorated. Since that can only be two commemorations, however, if there is both a II Vespers and a I Vespers to commemorate on Sunday, then the usual rules of concurrence given in the breviary will determine which one is commemorated.

In the event of an excepted feast, i.e., the feast of the first or second class rank, falling on a Sunday and taking precedence, then beginning on Sunday, the Sunday is commemorated as usual. The feast, of course, takes precedence at Vespers on Sunday, which is the feast's II Vespers, but Compline of a feast of the first or second class rank is always said of Sunday anyway according to the rubrics. It can get confusing when discussed in the abstract such as in these notes, but is usually quite clear when actually consulting the liturgical calendar for a given day to determine commemorations.

MATINS

Matins begins with the Triple Prayer, i.e, the Pater, Ave, and Credo. When that or the Dual Prayer are said before the offices, it is customary for those in the choir to make a profound reverence throughout. The traditional way of ensuring uniformity is for everyone to place their hands on their knees. Upon completing, when everyone has risen, the officiant begins the office. At the words "Domine labia mea aperies," it is optional, but traditional to make the sign of the cross over one's lips with the right thumb. Then the office continues as given in the breviary.

For the Invitatory, it is chosen according to the type of office as appointed in the rubrics and the liturgical calendar. The Invitatory as given for the day of the week is only used during masses of the season throughout the year. For offices said of saints, regardless of rank, the correct Invitatory is appointed is used. This is then sung by the cantor as appointed, and the choir sings Psalm 95 with the Invitatory woven into it as indicated, all standing. Thereafter, still standing, the choir sings the appointed hymn according to season. For excepted feasts, i.e., feasts of the first and second class, regardless of season or nature of the feast, the hymn appointed for the given day of the week throughout the year is used. (For example, a feast on a Wednesday during Lent would use the Wednesday hymn, not the Lenten hymn.)

Next, the choir sits for the Psalms, which begin a section of the office called the Nocturn. It is not uncommon, however, for the cantor to remain standing at least at the beginning if not throughout, for he must begin the antiphon. Here, the antiphon is according to season. Note, however, that for a feast of the first or second class, the Psalms of Sunday are always used regardless of season. The Psalms are sung as a group, with a single Gloria Patri at the end (except during offices of the season during Passiontide), and then the antiphon is sung again.

An additional note on antiphons for all offices:

In all offices, the antiphon is chosen according to season. Throughout the year, it is according to the day of the week. For a feast of the first or second class, the Psalms of Sunday are always used in all offices, but instead the antiphon as provided for feast of saints of first or second class is instead used. The exception to this is if the feast in question is of Our Lord, in which case it is the antiphon of Sunday that is used. During certain seasons, feasts, or octaves, an antiphon is specified. The antiphon for the season specified, then, is used, even on feasts. The exception to this is during Lent. During Lent, a feast is said as if it were not during Lent, i.e., the non-penitential version of the Psalms are used at Lauds, the preces are said standing, etc. Therefore, the choice of antiphon is according to the day of the week or, as previously explained, the version for first or second class feasts. Yet in other seasons, for example, Christmastide until the Epiphany, the seasonal antiphon is used even on feasts (excepting those of first or second class rank).

The Nocturn continues with a lesson. The longest lessons of all offices are found in Matins. Whoever will sing or read the lesson goes to the officiant, makes a profound reverence, and requests the blessing as given in the breviary. The officiant gives the blessing as specified, with the reader/lector making the sign of the cross on himself. Only a foremost who is a priest or another cleric to whom the faculty has been given makes the sign of the cross directly over the lector.

The lector then sings the lesson, standing, ending it as all lessons during the offices. The choir then makes the usual response as given in the breviary. Thus concludes the Nocturn.

The Nocturn is followed by the Te Deum, otherwise known as the Ambrosian Hymn. This is as always omitted in penitential seasons at offices of the season. However, it is still sung in penitential seasons if there is a feast of sufficient rank to take precedence over the day of the season. The choir stands during the Te Deum.

After the Te Duem, the Collect is sung. If the officiant is a cleric than the salutation Dominus vobiscum is used as usual. The otherwise the alternative is used as given. During the Collect, the officiant only uses the orans position, i.e., arms extended, if he is a priest.

As given in the rubrics, the Collect of the Day is sung by the foremost according to the day in the liturgical calendar. No commemorations are made.

Here the office should immediately proceed to Lauds. In the event that it does not, however, then the conclusion of the office follows as given in the breviary, with the final Pater as usual.

LAUDS

Lauds typically follows immediately after Matins without break. In that case, since they are treated as a single office, the Dual Prayer before Lauds is omitted, proceeding immediately to the opening versicles. If Lauds is said as a completely separate office, however, then the Dual Prayer is said in the usual manner.

After the Opening Versicles, the choir sits as usual for the Psalms. The principles for the antiphons are the same as given in Matins, and the same for all offices. Lauds, along with Vespers, have the lengthiest Psalter. The cantor and choir sing the Psalms as usual (see Matins).

In the Psalter of Lauds, however, there are two versions. The regular version, sometimes called Lauds I, is used outside Lent. This will be seen in the Sunday Psalter as an option. For the other days of the week, the Psalter as given is used outside Lent. Within the penitential season of Lent, for the offices of the season, Lauds II is used. That is, on Sunday, the version given for Lent, beginning with the Psalm Miserere me, is used. For the other days of the week, for offices of the season during Lent, the first Psalm given for any given day is replaced with the first Psalm provided for Sunday during Lent, i.e., the Miserere me. Then the remainder of the Psalter continues.

And note that for solemn recitations of Lauds, bishops wear the cappa magna (as well as through Matins before, with the hood up) until the Psalter in Lauds. During the singing of the Psalms, the Bishop changes from the cappa magna into the cope and stole in the colour of the day, taking the mitre, as given in the ceremonial for bishops.

Likewise, all other clerics who are officiating, to include the lector and cantor, at solemn Lauds may wear a cope, without stole, in the colour of the day. However, a priest who is officiating wears the stole with the cope. The biretta is used by all clerics, as is the zucchetto.

Laity who are officiating at solemn Lauds may also wear the cope, but always without stole, biretta, or zucchetto.

After the Psalter, the lector sings the chapter for the day as provided. This simply follows the day of the week unless, of course, it is an "excepted feast," i.e., a feast of the first or second class. In that case, as in all offices, the chapter of Sunday is read. And, as given in the rubrics in the breviary, the chapter ends, as always, with the usual response "But thou, O Lord have mercy on us." The lector stands during the chapter, but the choir continues to sit.

The chapter is followed by one of two hymns as provided, sung by the choir standing. The two hymns are the Benedicite omnia opera Domini and the Benedictus es Domine. The determination of which will be used is made by the foremost in the choir or other authority. It is not tied to the liturgical calendar. Note that in the Benedicite it is possible to shorten it, as given the rubrics, by omitting either section 2 or section 3, but not both.

The choir remains standing after the hymn for the preces. The exception to this is on certain ferial days, specifically those of Advent and Lent, Ember Days, all unprivileged vigils, and any offices of the dead – in which case the preces are said kneeling as given in the rubrics. In Lauds, however, the preces are admitted on feasts of double rank or higher. Regarding Sundays of higher rank, note that they are appointed in the liturgical calendar to be said as a semi-double, and therefore the preces are still said on those days.

The versicles are said by the foremost, and the responses by the choir as usual. The foremost begins the Pater as given, and then the rest is said silently by everyone until the foremost audibly finishes it with the final versicle as given. Then the versicles and responses continue.

If the preces are omitted, then the salutation in the usual manner before the Collect is still said – either the Dominus vobiscum or the Domine exaudi, according to the grade of the foremost. Then follows the Collect of the day, which is found in the section for Matins. At Lauds, there may be a commemoration according to the rules. In the event of the commemoration specified in the liturgical calendar, that collect is then sung after the Collect of the day. However, only two collects are permitted. Therefore, the second Collect of higher rank or precedence is used. In Lent and Advent, since the feria must be commemorated, it is the Collect of the feria that is used, with the commemoration of the Saint specified in the liturgical calendar omitted. Also, should both the primary collect and the commemoration be of saints for whom one of the general collects of saints is used, then it is only said once and not repeated. If the general collect that makes mention of the name of the saint is used, then the names of all Saints specified may be included in the single collect.

Here the office is concluded as given in the breviary. As usual, the Dominus vobiscum is replaced with the Domine exaudi if the foremost is not a cleric. At the Fidelium animae, all make the sign of the cross on themselves.

In the event that another office will not follow immediately, then the choir says, standing, a silent Pater noster. Then the foremost pronounces the versicle as given, with all making the sign of the cross on themselves. That is the signal to kneel for the final antiphon of the Blessed Virgin. The exception to this is during Paschaltide, during which the choir stands always for the final antiphon.

The antiphon is said in unison by the choir. Then the foremost says the versicle as given, with all making the sign of the cross on themselves. At this point, the prayer known as the Sacrosanctae may be said, kneeling, as an act of reparation for any small mistakes made during the recitation of the offices. It is entirely optional, and it may be said after any of the offices.

In the event that another office will immediately follow Lauds, however, the final Pater and the rest that follows is omitted, including the Marian antiphon. Instead the next office (Prime) begins with the Triple Prayer.

PRIME

Prime, being the office of the first hour, is one of the two offices that begins with the Triple Prayer. Its opening versicles are as usual, and they are followed by the hymn as provided in the breviary, with the choir standing. At the doxology at the end of the hymn, it is optional according to local custom to bow. For example, for the hymn in Prime, the Jam lucis, the doxology is the portion beginning "All laud...".

Then follows the Psalter as usual, noting that the antiphons are never doubled.

The Psalter is followed by the Chapter the usual manner. In Prime, the Chapter is followed by a Brief Respond, which is said standing. This is the same throughout the year except for Paschaltide. The foremost, as usual, begins the versicle. Here as always, the choir bows for the versicle of the Gloria Patri.

Next follow the Preces, which are always included in this office. As usual, they are said standing unless the preces were said kneeling at Lauds, in which case they are said kneeling as well. In other words, however the Preces were said (or would have been said in the case that they are omitted) at Lauds defines how they are said in other offices throughout the day. If they are said standing, then they are called Dominical Preces. If they are said kneeling, then they are called Ferial Preces.

Note that the Pater is begun by the foremost and then said silently as usual, and the same is done for the Credo. The Preces are followed by the General Confession. The various options based on whether one is saying this office communally or privately on one's own, as well as the state of the foremost, are provided in the breviary. The foremost says the Confiteor, and then the choir responds with the Misereatur. The choir then says the Confiteor, with the foremost following with the Misereatur and the Indulgentiam. All make the sign of the cross as given for the latter. In the event that the foremost is a priest, then he makes the sign of the cross in the usual manner over the choir. Otherwise, even if a cleric, he makes the sign of the cross over himself. The choir remains standing throughout all of the preceding.

Then there are several versicles and responses, followed by the Collect of the office, which never changes. The concluding versicles are said, and then follows immediately the Capitular Office.

The Capitular Office begins with a reading by the lector from the martyrology. In the event that the martyrology is not available, particularly in private recitations on one's own, then one meditates on the saints known to be for the day from the liturgical calendar and continues with the versicle.

When reading the martyrology, note that it is "antici-pated." That is, it is read according to the following day. So, if it is 3 March, then the martyrology for 4 March will be read. This provides an early preparation and reminder for what the next day will be liturgically. This is also for the following reason: if the following day will be a feast of a saint, the feast will actually begin with its I Vesper on the current day.

After the martyrology and its versicle and response, there is a collect sung by the foremost, which never varies. Then the typical opening versicles and responses are said as given three times, followed by a series of other versicles and responses and a Collect, which also never varies. All of this is said standing (and here as well as elsewhere in these notes, "said" and "sung" are used interchangeably, for the offices may be either said or sung).

Then the choir sits. The lector goes to the foremost as given in Matins and asks for the blessing, using the formula as provided in the breviary. And here as usual, if the foremost is a priest or else a cleric with the faculty, the sign of the cross is made during this blessing over the lector.

The lector, standing, reads the Brief Lesson, which is always the same. At this point, all stand for the conclusion, which is given in the breviary. The two signs of the cross indicated are made by everyone over themselves in all cas-es. Then, as usual, follows the silent Pater Noster, unless another office will follow.

TERCE

Terce, being the office of the third hour (mid-morning), begins as usual with the Dual Prayer and opening versi-cles, followed by a hymn, sung by all standing. Then follows the Psalter in the usual manner, with the choir sitting. The antiphons are never doubled. Next the lector reads the chapter.

The preces are never said in Terce except as provided in the rubrics. That is, they are said only on the ferial days of Advent and Lent, Ember Days, all unprivileged vigils, and in the offices of the dead. Thus if they are said, they are always said kneeling.

At this point the choir stands (unless the preces were said, and which case they remain kneeling, though the foremost stands as always here), and the foremost sings the Collect of the day. There are no commemorations at the little hours.

The office concludes as usual, with the choir standing. Unless another office will follow, then as usual, the silent Pater is said, and the choir departs.

SEXT

Sext, the office of the sixth hour (midday), follows the same basic format as Terce. Although the content is different, since the structure is the same, then all that was given above for Terce applies here.

NONE

None, the office of the ninth hour (mid-afternoon), likewise follows the same basic format as Terce and Sext.

VESPERS

Vespers, the sunset office, is one of the major hours. Like Lauds, it may also be said in a solemn fashion, and so what was described in the general notes for solemn Lauds applies for Vespers.

Vespers begins with the Dual Prayer and the opening versicles as usual. It immediately proceeds to the Psalter, with antiphon according to the usual rules. Antiphons are doubled if the office is of double rank or higher. And as usual, the choir sits during the Psalms. If the foremost is a bishop, and Vespers is being sung solemnly, then he changes as previously described from the cappa magna into the cope during the Psalms.

The Psalter is followed by the Chapter, which is sung by the lector in the usual manner. The lector stands, while the choir remains seated.

Then the choir stands for the hymn, which is the Phos hilaron. However, another hymn may be substituted with episcopal permission, according to the rubrics of the breviary, as appropriate. If that is done, it will typically be for a public service and may relate to a particular feast or special occasion. Typically it would not be substituted.

Next comes the great Canticle of Mary that is a highlight of Vespers, the Magnificat. The choir remains standing. The cantor intones the antiphon, which is according to season. During all of Paschaltide, it is always the one given for that season. However, given the principle that feasts during Lent and Advent are exempted from the penitential character, the antiphon for that season is not used, but rather that which is given for the day of the week throughout the year. Since there is no antiphon specifically provided for first or second class feasts here, then following the standard principles of the breviary, the one for Sunday is used.

Also, it is optional according to local use to make the sign of the cross over oneself at the very beginning, i.e., at "My soul doth magnify…". And, as always, the choir bows at the end during the Gloria Patri, except that it is always omitted during offices of the season during Passiontide.

Like at Lauds, the preces during Vespers are omitted on feasts of Double rank or above – except that, of course, during Vespers of Sundays of higher rank that are appointed in the liturgical calendar to be said in the offices as semi-doubles, the preces are still said. And, the standard rules regarding standing or kneeling apply.

Next follows the Collect of the day and, if one is appointed, a single commemoration as described during Lauds. The Collect is then followed by the concluding versicles as usual. Then follows, unless Compline will follow immediately, the silent Pater and the Marion Antiphon.

COMPLINE

Compline is the completion of the offices, and it is the one office that does not begin with either the Triple or Dual Prayer. Instead, the lector goes to the foremost and requests a blessing in the usual manner as given in the breviary. The choir sits, and the lector stands while singing the Lesson, which is always the same. Indeed, with the exception of some minor changes based on season, and the Psalms, Compline is always identical.

After the Lesson, all stand, and the foremost continues with the versicle as given; a silent Pater Noster is said, and then the General Confession is said as provided in Prime. Afterwards the opening versicles are said, which differ slightly. At the Converte nos, all make the sign of the cross over the left breast with the right thumb.

The choir sits, and the Psalms are sung as usual. The antiphons are never doubled. Then the choir stands for the hymn, which is always the Te lucis ante terminum as given in the breviary. This is followed by the Little Chapter and Brief Respond. The choir sits during the chapter, while the lector stands. All stand for the Brief Respond. It is always the same except during Paschaltide, and of course the Gloria Patri is omitted during Passiontide.

The choir remained standing for the Gospel Canticle. The cantor intones the antiphon, and then the choir continues with the Nunc Dimittis.

The Preces follow, and they are always included. They are said standing unless they were appointed to be kneeling at Lauds. Then follows the Collect, which never varies, recited by the foremost. Next the office concludes with the versicle given. All make the sign of the cross over themselves. The one exception is that if the foremost is a priest or a cleric with the faculty, then he may make the sign of the cross in the usual manner here over the choir.

The Fidelium animae is not said. Rather, the choir immediately kneels, except in Paschaltide, and begins with the Marion antiphon directly without the usual preceding Pater, versicle, and response. Then the Triple Prayer is said as usual, standing. Note that this is the final act of the office cycle for the day. Therefore, even if Matins for the following day will follow immediately, the Triple Prayer is still said twice – once at the end of Compline and once at the beginning of Matins.

VIGIL OFFICE

In the Patriarchate there exists an indult for a public liturgy known as a vigil office. This is typically something that could be done for a major feast. Since the feast begins at I Vespers the preceding day, the Vigil Office begins at that time. The office simply consists of I Vespers, Compline, Matins, and Lauds beginning in the evening and then said in continuous sequence, one immediately following the other.

DIVINE OFFICE OF THE DEAD

The Divine Office of the Dead is an office unto itself. On days on which the mass/office of the dead is appointed, and also on days of ferial or simple rank on which the dead will be commemorated, this office may be set in place of Vespers that day. Otherwise it must be said separately from other offices, though it may follow an office immediately.

As given in the rubrics, the Dual Prayer is not said. All stand for the opening versicle and then sit for the Psalms. The Gloria Patri is obviously omitted, and there are no antiphons.

The Magnificat then follows, with all standing. All then kneel for the versicles, responses, and orations that follow.

Then all sit for the First and Second Lessons, except for the lector, who stands as usual. All rise for the Third Lesson, which is the Gospel Lesson. However, there is neither an introduction nor a salutation.

Next all stand for the Conclusion. The Conclusion is led by the foremost. At that point, the office ends, and nothing else is said.

Vesture for the Divine Office of the Dead is choir dress as usual. However, the cope may be used in the same manner as prescribed for Lauds and Vespers if the office will be said solemnly. Bishops arriving in the cappa magna with the hood up over the head will then change into the cope, stole, and simplex mitre during the beginning Psalms. The cope is always black, or, if a black cope is not available, then purple. White is only used in the event of an office said for a young child under the age of innocence for whom the requiem rites would be permitted in white.

TENEBRAE

During the Sacred Triduum, additional offices of Matins and Lauds are provided in the breviary. These are optional. However, as given in the general rubrics of the breviary, if the full ritual of Tenebrae is to be observed, including the extinguishing of candles, then the full form of those offices must be used. If those offices are used, then they take the place of the regular Matins and Lauds for the day. However, if they will not be used, then the regular offices of Matins and Lauds in the breviary are used.

COLOURS USED DURING PAPAL MASSES

1. Masses celebrated by the Archfather or else presided by the Archfather in grand choral habit used only two colours, red or white, in accordance with the colours associated with St. Stephen and ancient Byzantine custom.

2. Gold or silver may substitute for white. Red is used when the specified liturgical colour is red, purple, rose, or black. White, gold, or silver is used when the specified colour is white or green.

3. All wearing liturgical vestments wear the same colour.

4. If a mass is presided over by the Archfather in grand choral habit or mozzetta, then the usual liturgical colour as prescribed in the Ordo Calendar and rubrics is used by the

Sacred Ministers, but the Archfather uses only red or white as appropriate to the liturgy.

REQUIREMENT OF CLERGY TO RECITE THE DIVINE OFFICES

Motu Proprio of 1 September A.D. 2012 - APS 2:8

The requirement for clergy, both regular and secular, and members of religious orders to recite the Divine Offices in the Breviary is herewith amended as follows:

1. All Bishops, Priests, Deacons, and Sub-Deacons are obligated to recite daily the offices of Lauds, Vespers, and Compline, except when impeded by lawful or just cause. However, it is still commendatory to recite Matins and one or more of the Little Hours when possible.

2. Members of religious orders shall recite the Divine Offices according to the rules set forth by the religious order, which shall include the offices of Lauds, Vespers, and Compline.

3. Lauds, Vespers, and Compline from the Anglican Breviary are particularly encouraged for public worship of the faithful.

4. It is reaffirmed that the daily offices contained within the 2010 Anglo-Catholic Book of Common Prayer are principally intended for the use of the laity and do not suffice for the obligation of the clergy mentioned in No. 1 above and in Canon Law to recite the Divine Offices. However, they may be used for public worship of the faithful.

5. The Roman Breviary, namely the breviary equivalent to the Anglican Breviary in general form, but in Latin and used according to specific Roman rubrics, may be used for private devotions of the clergy to fulfill their obligation, and by the faithful. The offices, then, in private recitation may be according to either the Roman rubrics as given in the Roman breviary or the Anglican rubrics as given in the Anglican breviary and the instructions of the Patriarchal See. Furthermore, the Divine Offices of the Anglican Breviary, when said as public liturgy, may use, in whole or in part, the Latin equivalent from the Roman Breviary. In

such cases, the rubrics of the Anglican Breviary and of this Particular Church are followed.

Given at the Court of Saint Mary of Walsingham this 1ˢᵗ day of September in the 2012ᵗʰ year of the Incarnation.

USE OF LATIN IN THE DIVINE OFFICES

Rescriptum

1 November A.D. 2015

For the benefit of maintaining our Anglo-Roman liturgy that so beuatifully demonstrates the nature of our See's heritage, the following regulations are clarified for the inclusion of Latin into the recitation of the Divine Offices.

1. The Psalter, when chanted, is sung in Latin as given in the Liber Usualis or another suitable setting. When so used, the Gloria Patri and the Antiphons are likewise sung in Latin. This likewise applies to the Hymns and Canticles.

2. The Lessons and their responses are recited in English, and likewise are the Chapters and their Brief Responds. In sing offices, they may chanted in English or Latin.

3. The salutations and, where relevant, preceding versicle, viz., Domine exaudi orationem meam and Dominus vobiscum and their respective responses, as well as Oremus may be in Latin, but the Collects are in liturgical English (and hereafter all references to English are specifically refer to liturgical English). If Latin is used for part of the salutation, it must be used for all of it, e.g., if Dominus vobiscum is in Latin, then so must Oremus and Domine exaudi orationem meam be in Latin.

4. The Dual and Triple Prayers may be in Latin, as may be the instances of the Pater Noster and Confiteor within the Offices.

5. The Opening Versicles for all offices may be in Latin, but if they are, then they must be entirely in Latin, including the Gloria Patri.

6. In the Preces and in series of versicles and responses, the first versicles and corresponding responses and/or the last

versicles and corresponding responses may be in Latin if they are of "common forms," e.g., the Kyrie Eleison, the Pater Noster, the Confiteor, Adjutorium nostrum etc., the Domine exaudi orationem meam, the Creed, and the Dominus vobiscum. All versicles and their corresponding responses within the Preces otherwise are in English – except that, if they are sung, then they may be sung in either English or Latin.

7. Collects are both recited and chanted in English. For commemorations, the antiphon and versicle and response are typically both recited and chanted in English.

8. The closing versicles of the offices may be in Latin, but if they are, then they likewise must all be. The Final Antiphons of the Blessed Virgin may be in Latin or English, but the collect is entirely in English.

9. In Matins, the Absolutions and Benedictions are given in English.

10. During the Capitular Office of Prime, the martyrology and its following versicle and response are typically in English. The collect that follows is in English. The versicles and responses that follow may be in English or Latin through the end of the Pater Noster, but as usual, if Latin is used in that section, then it must be used for all parts of said section. Then, the Gloria Patri and Oremus may be in English or Latin, followed by the Collect in English. Finally, following the Brief Lesson of the Capitular Office, the versicles and responses, as well as the benediction, may be either entirely in English or entirely in Latin.

11. During Compline, the initial benediction is said in English. The Lesson may be in English or Latin, but in either case Deo gratias may be said in English or Latin according to custom. The following versicle, Pater, etc. through the opening versicles may be either entirely in English or entirely in Latin. The Preces, if they are said, may be said entirely in English or else in Latin from the Kyrie through the Creed, and then again from the Domine exaudi through Oremus. The Collect is in English as usual. Then the closing versicles as usual may be entirely in English or entirely in Latin.

12. When reciting or singing offices of the dead, in the Preces of Vespers and Lauds, the versicles may either be said entirely in English or else in Latin, but only the Pater at the beginning and then again from the Requiem aeternam through Oremus. Then, likewise, the closing versicles may be entirely in English or entirely in Latin.

FORM OF THE PRAYERS AT THE FOOT OF THE ALTAR

Taken from the
Motu Proprio of 27 September A.D. 2015 - APS 5:5

The Celebrant says his own *Confiteor* and then the *Misereatur*, using, in English, the plural *you* forms, and in Latin, the plural *vestri* forms. The full plural form in Latin is:

Misereatur vestri omnipotens Deus, et dimissis peccatis vestris, perducat vos ad vitam aeternam.

However, when there is only one server, the priest uses precisely the same *Misereatur* form as said by the server, i.e., with the singular *tui* form.

When reciting the mass without servers, the *Misereatur* is recited, in English, with the plural *our* forms, and in Latin, the plural *nostri* forms. The full plural form in Latin when reciting the Holy Mass alone is:

Misereatur nostri omnipotens Deus, et dimissis peccatis nostris, perducat nos ad vitam aeternam.

REQUIREMENT FOR PRIESTS TO CELEBRATE THE MASS

Motu Proprio of 2 September A.D. 2012 - APS 2:8

The requirement for priests to celebrate the Holy Sacrifice of the Mass under Canon Law is herewith amended as follows:

1. All priests shall celebrate the Holy Mass at least once per week, unless impeded by just or lawful cause. However, more frequent celebration of the Holy Mass is to be highly commended.

2. The weekly mass to be said should ordinarily be on a Sunday. However, if appointed ecclesiastical duty requires that a given priest assist at Sunday mass, and there is no additional public mass for him to celebrate, then he may either celebrate a private mass that day (if he did not receive the Sacrament at the mass at which he assisted), or he may celebrate another mass on another day during the week.

3. All priests shall celebrate the Holy Mass on Holy Days of Obligation, and this shall be in addition to the requirement to celebrate weekly mass.

Given at the Court of Saint Mary of Walsingham this 2nd *day of September in the* 2012th *year of the Incarnation.*

INDULT FOR TRANSFERENCE OF FEASTS FOR PASTORAL REASONS

confirmed by Instruction, 1 October 2010

Feasts are encouraged to be kept on their proper day. However, there may arise cases in which, for the good of the faithful, the feasts should be transferred. The permissible transferences are as follows:

1. Feasts of any rank falling on a day not Sunday may be transferred to another day not Sunday within the same week, provided that the feast being transferred has rank equal to or greater than the rank of the day to which it is being transferred. The feast, if any, and all commemorations (if any) of the day to which the transferred feast is being transferred, should be commemorated.

2. The following feasts may be transferred to the preceding or following Sunday: The Most Sacred Heart of Jesus (to the following Sunday only) and other First and Second Class feasts of our Lord; First or Second Class feasts of the Blessed Virgin; the principal patron saint or saints of a particular church, parish or diocese; the dedication or anni-

versary of dedication of a particular church; Holy Days of Obligation other than Good Friday and Christmas. Feasts may not be transferred to Sundays of the First Class or to Sundays on which is appointed by the calendar a feast with rank Double of the First Class. The Sunday is commemorated.

Update by Directive of 2015 (APS 5:5): The provision of transferring feasts of Our Lord as indicated in the Directive of 1 October 2010 does not apply to feasts of Our Lord as provided in the Proper of the Season, such as the Epiphany. Furthermore, when the observation of a feast with an octave is transferred, the octave remains in its regular place in the calendar, i.e., it is only the celebration of the principle feast that is moved. Likewise, no feast that has an octave with a specific mass for the Sunday within the Octave should be transferred, but such feasts should be always kept on their proper days.

3.   If a feast with an octave is transferred according to rule No. 2 above, the octave remains in its usual position, i.e., the octave does not move, but only the day within the octave on which the feast itself is observed.

INDULT FOR VOTIVE MASSES
OF THE MOST BLESSED SACRAMENT

confirmed by Instruction, 1 October 2010

During the seven days following the Feast of Corpus Christi, if the procession of the Most Blessed Sacrament is to occur on those days, then on such days the Votive Mass of the Most Blessed Sacrament may be said as a Votive Mass of the Second Class.

INDULT FOR SATURDAY MASSES
OF THE BLESSED VIRGIN MARY

confirmed by Instruction, 1 October 2010

One Saturday mass of the Blessed Virgin Mary per month per parish may be said as a votive mass with rank of second class.

INDULT FOR FRIDAY MASSES
OF THE SACRED HEART, HOLY CROSS, AND
PASSION OF OUR LORD JESUS CHRIST

confirmed by Instruction, 1 October 2010

One mass of the Sacred Heart may be celebrated with rank of third class on the first Friday of each month. One mass of either the Holy Cross or the Passion of Our Lord Jesus Christ may be celebrated with third class rank on other Fridays during the month. These masses are permitted one per parish.

INDULT FOR THURSDAY MASSES
OF OUR LORD JESUS CHRIST
SUPREME AND ETERNAL PRIEST

confirmed by Instruction, 1 October 2010

One mass of the Sacred Heart may be celebrated with rank of third class on any Thursday during a month.

INDULT FOR THE MASS
OF OUR LADY OF WALSINGHAM

confirmed by Instruction, 1 October 2010

As medieval patroness of England and modern patroness of all English-speaking peoples, this feast is of particular importance. This feast may be kept on its usual day, the 25th of March, the Feast of the Annunciation. Our Lady of Walsingham may simply be remembered on this day or commemorated at the mass of the Annunciation using the collect from the Common of the Blessed Virgin Mary, or with a separate mass using the Common of the Blessed Virgin Mary.

SACRED MUSIC

All music used in high or sung masses, or superimposed at a low mass must be directed towards the common act of worship. The choir may sing the propers in their appropriate time, or else substitute a hymn or anthem of an appropriate topic and form. In a low mass, music may be used, but the propers are not sung.

MUSIC FOR HIGH AND SUNG MASSES

ASPERGES AND INTROIT

There may be a hymn of procession before the *Asperges*. The *Asperges* is sung, and then followed by the Introit or some other suitable hymn.

KYRIE AND GLORIA

The *Kyrie* is sung following the Summary of the Law. If the setting is long, the priest may retire to sit at the sedilia. The priest intones the *Gloria* from the altar. If it is a long setting, the ministers and he may, as with the *Kyrie*, return to the sedilia. If he sings the *Kyrie* or *Gloria* with the congregation, though, he remains at the altar.

GRADUAL

The gradual hymn is sung in preparation for the Gospel. It may be sung according to the propers of the mass being said, or another hymn or anthem may be used.

CREED

If the *Creed* is sung, then the ministers may, as with the *Kyrie*, return to the sedilia. If they sing the *Creed* with the congregation, though, they remains at the altar.

SANCTUS AND BENEDICTUS

These are either sung without pause, or the *Benedictus* follows the consecration. No singing or music of any kind is permitted during the consecration. The choir and/or congregation sing the *Sanctus* and *Benedictus* while the priest begins the Canon.

AGNUS DEI

The priest does not return to the sedilia during the *Agnus Dei*.

COMMUNION HYMN

The appointed communion hymn in the propers, or some other suitable hymn, should be sung after the General Thanksgiving. Alternatively, the hymn may be sung during communion.

USE OF RECORDED SACRED MUSIC

by Patriarchal Instruction on Saturday within
the Octave of Corpus Christi
9 *June A.D.* 2012 - APS 2:5

1) Sacred Music used in the Liturgy and Extra-liturgical devotions of the Church, including processions, must be for the purpose of enhancing the worship of God by the faithful. Music itself forms an offering of the people to God. It must never be entertainment. While it is ideal that all music in Sacred Worship be sung live during said worship, it is acknowledged and understood that the purpose of sacred music may be equally well-served through the use of pre-recorded Sacred Music in certain circumstances where a suitable live choir or cantor cannot reasonably be obtained. It is further acknowledged that the recorded music is itself a work of human beings which is capable of being used repeatedly for a worthy purpose, just as a sacred painting is the work of an artist and may be used repeatedly to draw people towards God.

2) Pre-recorded music must be equivalent to that which would be sung by the choir. This includes the appropriate endings, doxologies, antiphons, etc. appropriate to the liturgical season and day. It must further be dignified in nature and used for the purpose of enhancing the worship of those present.

3) Only for the music of the Holy Mass, Divine Office, or extra-liturgical services that would be sung by the choir or a cantor may pre-recorded music be sung. Those parts as-

signed to the Celebrant, Sacred Ministers, or others outside the choir during the Holy Mass, or to the Foremost at the Divine Offices must not be recorded, but must be sung by the appropriate living person present.

4) It is well-known that when the choir sings a given part of the liturgy of the Holy Mass, the Celebrant nevertheless is responsible for saying it as well. Likewise, if recorded music is used, the Celebrant must say the required parts of the liturgy.

5) The use of pre-recorded music must never allow worship to become distracted or to become passive. This equally applies to live music. Indeed, all music used in the liturgy must be used for the enhancement of the worship of God. While a device for playing recorded music cannot itself worship God, it may be used as a tool for the enhancement of the worship of God by living persons present.

6) The mere listening to pre-recorded music does not constitute participation in the liturgy, just as the mere listening to live music does not constitute participation in the liturgy.

7) The provisions of this instruction apply only to those cases in which dignified live music of a quality suitable for public worship cannot reasonably be obtained.

COMMUNION AT AN PAPAL MASS
OF HIGHEST SOLEMNITY

As defined and confirmed from ancient tradition in motu proprio of 23 August A.D. 2020 (APS 10:5)

RVTHERFORDVS PP. I

MOTU PROPRIO

The altar should be prepared with two purificators, with a third at the credence table.

After the Prayers of peace, the Archfather goes to the throne in the usual manner and sits wearing the mitre. A server follows, carrying the fistula and a second chalice, using the humeral veil. A server also takes a third purificator to the throne.

The Deacon of the Mass then takes the paten with the host and gives it to the Sub-Deacon of the Mass. An asterisk may be placed on the paten by the Deacon. The Deacon then placed a richly embroidered pall upon the chalice and take it in both hands. Without genuflecting, the Deacon (first) and the Sub-Deacon (following) proceed to the throne. At that point, the Archfather gives up the mitre and stands.

And note that all that is appointed for the Deacon and Sub-Deacon may, if the mass be a sung mass rather than a high mass, be done by any cleric otherwise qualified for the position. In that case, they ought still to be vested in dalmatic and tunicle, but over a rochet or surplice as appropriate rather than an alb, and without stole and maniple. Also note that most traditionally these offices are served by members of the Patriarchal Chapter.

The Archfather recites the usual prayer and takes the paten, without the asterisk (which is removed by the Sub-Deacon). Taking the host and paten in the left hand as usual, he recites the Domine non sum signus. The bells are not rung. He then consumes the smaller of the two halves of the host in the usual manner and returns the remaining host and paten to the Sub-Deacon.

The Assistant Priest takes the fistula from the server and hands it to the Archfather. The Deacon removes the pall and holds the chalice. The Archfather inserts the fistula and receives some of the Precious Blood. The pall is handed to a server, and the Deacon retrieves the Chalice, with the fistula still in it.

The Archfather again takes the paten and breaks the host into two pieces. He communicates the Deacon, who remains standing holding the chalice, in the usual manner. He then communicates the Sub-Deacon, who kneels.

The Deacon and Sub-Deacon return to the altar without genuflecting. The Deacon places the chalice on the corporal, and the Sub-Deacon places the paten on the corporal. The Deacon then purifies the fistula with a purificator and, wrapping it in the purificator, gives it to a server to return to the credence table. The Sub-Deacon then purifies the paten over the chalice with the second purificator. The Deacon consumes the remainder of the Precious Blood, as well as the particle therein. He then recites the prayers and carries out the ablutions in the usual manner, assisted by the Sub-Deacon.

If there is to be no Communion of Clergy and Congregation

Meanwhile, the Archfather, still standing at the throne, purifies his fingers over the second chalice in the usual manner. The chalice is taken back to the credence table. Mass continues at the throne as usual.

If there will be Communion of Clergy and Congregation

After the Deacon and Sub-Deacon go to the altar, the Archfather takes the ciborium, which has been brought to the throne by the Assistant Priest, and recites the Ecce Agnus Dei in the usual manner. The priest or priests who will distribute communion then begin the distribution. They should be vested in surplice and take the stole for the distribution only. If they are prelates of any rank, they take the surplice or cotta over the rochet and then take the stole over that, having laid aside any choral vesture. They return to their previous vesture after communion.

Meanwhile, the Archfather, still standing at the throne, purifies his fingers over the second chalice in the usual manner. The chalice is taken back to the credence table. Mass continues at the throne as usual.

MELKITE AND EASTERN DEACONS DURING PAPAL MASSES OF HIGHEST SOLEMNITY

In recognition of the Byzantine and Slavic heritage of the Anglican Patriarchate comprise a valued and ancient part of its patrimony, and in recognition of the Melkite and Russian Rite apostolic succession of the patriarchate, at Patriarchal masses of the highest solemnity, two additional Deacons of the Mass may be op-tionally used. These deacons are known as the Melkite Deacon in the Eastern Deacon. If they are used, both may be used, or either one may be used.

If the deacon is of the specific rite or else biritual, then he vests as a deacon of that rite in the colour appropriate to the mass as usual. However, because of the patrimony and apostolic succession of the Anglican Patriarchate, any cleric of the patriarchate of the order of deacon or above may serve in these roles, in which case the vest in Latin vestments.

In procession, except where stated, the Melkite Deacon and East-ern Deacon follow in that order behind the Latin Deacon. During the mass, the deacons in general sit at the sedilia next to the Latin Dea-con and Sub-Deacon, with the Melkite to the right and otherwise stand likewise on either side of them, such as at the Prayers at the Foot of the Altar. At the Gospel, they go to the place where the gos-pel will be sung. It is first sung in Latin and then, if there is a Melkite Deacon, in Greek, and if there is an Eastern Deacon, then in Russian or another Slavic language. During the portions of the mass at the throne, the deacons sit with the Latin deacon of the mass. Dur-ing the portions of the mass at the altar, the deacons stand with the Latin Deacon of the Mass on the pavement or second altar step as usual. If there is only one such Deacon, he stands to the left of the Latin Deacon. If there are both of the deacons, then the Eastern Deacon stands to the left, and the Melkite Deacon stands to the right. When the Latin Deacon goes to the predella, he is accompanied by the other two, who stand to the outside, the Melkite Deacon closest to the Latin Deacon. During the communion at throne, the two dea-cons follow behind the Latin Deacon and Sub-Deacon, standing side-by-side behind them, the Melkite to the right. They then likewise follow back to the altar for the purification, standing side-by-side on the second step of the altar.

Patriarchal Motu Proprio
Regarding Penance, Fasting, & Abstinence
during Lent and on Ember Days

2018

S ACRIFICE is a key and essential theme of the Catholic Faith. We are invited by our Lord to take up our own crosses and follow Him. Indeed, at the Holy Sacrifice of the Mass, we take part in and unify ourselves to that very same true and living Sacrifice on the Cross. It is, therefore, right and proper that the Church has maintained a sense of penance and penitential acts throughout her history to the present.

In those acts of penance of the Church and her people, it is the intent that is of most importance. Indeed, a specific act may lose its purpose and therefore its merit and effect over time when the physical or temporal aspects change such that the underlying spiritual meaning is no longer so obviously taught. And, as taught in the Parable of the Pharisee and the Publican, it is possible to make great show of penance while being empty spiritually inside. Such acts are clearly of no avail.

We, therefore, affirm the spirit and intent of penance and sacrifice are the most important aspect relative to their form. We further recognise the long-standing traditions of this See and also take note of customs that prevail around the world, e.g., the permitting of chicken rather than fish on a Lenten Friday, given the relative expense in some areas of fish.

In the sovereign Imperial Patriarchate of St. Stephen and all her suffragan Sees, therefore, the following shall be imposed on Fridays of Lent, Ash Wednesday, and on Ember Days:

> 1. An act of self-denial, sacrifice, and penance shall be undertaken by all clergy and faithful. This act is of the choosing of the individual, provided it meets the spirit and intent of penance. Acts of charity towards others have always been the primary form of giving of one's self in sacrifice and penance within this See.

2.   The abstention from all flesh meat or of red meat, as well as fasting in its usual form, may, as a matter of tradition, be continued and undertaken as the act of self-denial, sacrifice, and penance, but is not required.

3.   The Patriarchal See, as well as jurisdictional bishops and superiors of religious communities and orders may impose specific acts of penance as deemed appropriate.

The requirement of penance is lifted, as in current use, under the following conditions:

1.   If a semi-double or greater feast falls on a Lenten Friday or Lenten Ember Day, excepting Good Friday, the requirement is lifted.

2.   If a feast falls on an Ember Day elsewhere in the liturgical year, the requirement is likewise lifted.

3.   The clergy and faithful are not required to take the exemption and may undertake their penance as they would otherwise do.

The provisions of this decree may be further applied to all Fridays during the year at individual or jurisdictional choice.

Given at the Court of St. Mary of Walsingham in the House of St. Stephen, this 18th day of September in the two thousand eighteenth year of the Incarnation.

Patriarchal Indult
2014

The tropical (summer) habit may be used beginning after Vespers on Saturday in White in areas that are geographically tropical or sub-tropical, or in which the temperature at this time reaches a high of over 80 degree Fahrenheit. In such areas the winter cappa magna is exchanged for the summer at Vespers on Saturday in White instead of at I Vespers of the Ascension, following the same procedure. However, if the weather is sufficiently warm to justify, then this habit may be used beginning at Vespers of Easter Vigil. Low Sunday is the preferred earliest time, however. The tropical habit is not used within the City of Rome. Also, even if the habit is changed on Saturday in White, the liturgy appointed for the various seasons does not change.

Patriarchal Directive

25 October A.D. 2014

In both Tropical and Sub-Tropical geographical areas, the tropical habits may be worn from the usual time until the start of the Winter Half-Year, i.e., First Vespers of the Feast of Saint Catherine, 25 November, provided the weather is suitably warm. In such areas in which the temperature remains consistently above 70 degrees Fahrenheit, the tropical habit may be worn year-round, but only with dispensation of the Patriarchal See.

Confirmation regarding the procedure in the event that the entire Triduum cannot be celebrated

Taken from the Caeremoniale Aulae Sanctae Mariae Walsinghamensis:

The Sacred Triduum is one continuous liturgy. It either must be celebrated in its entirety or not at all. However, Good Friday is a Holy Day of Obligation. If the Triduum cannot be celebrated in its entirety, then 1) the mass of Holy Thursday is not said; 2) the liturgy of Good Friday in the missal is said as given through the Veneration of the Cross inclusive, and there the liturgy ends; 3) the liturgy of Holy Saturday and the Easter Vigil are not said.

Clarification regarding the stripping of the Altar on Holy Thursday if the Triduum is not celebrated

If the full Triduum liturgy is not celebrated, the Offices naturally still take place, as said offices may be even private. Note that in the Mass of Holy Thursday, the altars are stripped before the Office of Vespers. Therefore, should the full liturgy not be performed, the altars are nevertheless stripped after None and before Vespers on the morning of Holy Thursday and remain thus until after None and before Vespers on the morning of Holy Saturday, being the first Office of Paschaltide.

Regarding Anticipated Offices during Lent

Beginning with Vespers on the firsr Saturday in Lent, Vespers is said before noon on every day of Lent, including feasts, excepting Sundays. Therefore, the following schedule is the standard, which may be modified slightly, but not to the point of violating the rubrics or the spirit of the offices. Note, therefore, that noon need not be absolutely precise, but approximate.

Friday before the First Sunday in Lent:

Vespers is said as usual in the evening. Matins and Lauds for *Saturday* are said after Compline in the evening of Friday.

Saturday before the First Sunday in Lent

Prime, Terce, Sext, and None are said in the morning as convenient (note that, with the "shifted" offices, Prime and Terce take during Lent the temporal place of Matins and Lauds throughout the year). Vespers is said before noon. Matins and Lauds of Sunday are said in the evening.

Sundays in Lent

Prime and Terce are said in the morning. The principal mass of the day is typically said after Terce. Sext and None are said in the afternoon. Vespers and Compline are said in the evening at their usual times. Matins and Lauds of Monday are said thereafter. Sundays, therefore, are a particularly appropriate time for the optional use of the Vigil Service, i.e., the sequential recitation of Vespers, Compline, Matins, & Lauds.

Feriae in Lent

Prime, Terce, Sext, and None are said in the morning as convenient (note that, with the "shifted" offices, Prime and Terce take during Lent the temporal place of Matins and

Lauds throughout the year). Vespers is said before noon. If it is a Saturday, then Matins and Lauds of Sunday are said in the evening.

Holy Saturday

Vespers follows the Easter Vigil as given in the missal and breviary. Compline is said in the late afternoon or early evening. Matins and Lauds of Easter Sunday are said in the evening.

Patriarchal Decree

From time to time it is the duty of a pastor to help those of his flock discern the truth of the Holy Catholic Faith from amidst the abounding confusion of today's secularized world. This applies no less to the confusion within Christ's Holy Church, which has suf-fered the influences of modernism and liberalism especially during the last several decades. The promulgation of the Novus Ordo through Catholic mass media, as well as it being the standard in the overwhelming majority of parishes in the world, have introduced confusion in both clergy and laity. We, therefore, in a sincere desire to avoid similar confusion within our See, decree the following:

1)   The clergy and laity under the pastoral care and authority of the Patriarchate of St. Stephen are absolutely prohibited from attending or participating in masses of the Novus Ordo, except as part of official diplomatic or ecumenical events. In such cases of attendance, the clergy is to observe proper clerical deportment, including the wearing of the clerical cassock; and the clergy and laity ought to refrain from reception of the Sacrament, given the grave doubts of the validity of the Novus Ordo by the words of Cardinals Ottaviani and Bacci in writing to His Holiness Pope Paul VI, and indeed of various statements by Paul VI himself, and also of Pope Saint Pius V and Pope Pius XII.

2)   The provisions of Canon 68 Sec. 1 of the Code of Particular Canon Law that permits, with the permission of the Patriarch, other traditional Roman liturgy to be celebrated by clergy of the Patriar-chate does not apply to the Novus

Ordo mass or Novus Ordo forms of any sacrament, for that would conflict with the requirement that such liturgy be traditional. Thus, the clergy of the Patriarchal See of St. Stephen, Anglican Rite Roman Catholic Church may not use the Novus Ordo form of any sacrament of the Holy Church, in whole or in part.

3)   Those in danger of death may, in cases of extreme need, receive the final sacraments from a Novus Ordo priest if none other is available.

4)   These provisions apply not only to the Novus Ordo of the Roman Rite, but the Novus Ordo of the other Rites within the Roman Communion and elsewhere.

5)   Likewise, these same provisions apply regarding attendance and participating in the rites of the Orthodox churches, as well as those of the Anglican Communion and, it need hardly be said, of Protes-tant Churches.

6)   Those of the clergy or laity who violate the terms of this decree without express *pro hac vice* permission of the Patriarch, will be subject to interdict *latae sententiae* and, for clergy, immediate suspension of all faculties, this interdict being reserved to the Patriarchal See.

Given at the Court of Saint Mary of Walsingham, this 23rd day of April, on the Feast of Saint George the Martyr, in the year our Lord 2016.

REGULATIONS PERTAINING TO THE 1928 B.C.P.

Patriarchal Letter
"On the Deficiencies of the
1928 Book of Common Prayer"
15 July A.D. 2012 - APS 2:7

To the Bishops and Regular Clergy of the Anglican Rite Roman Catholic Church,

The 1928 Book of Common Prayer (BCP) of the Protestant Episcopal Church has long been the staple of the liturgy for the groups of Anglicans known commonly as Continuing Anglicans, who separated from the same Protestant Episcopal Church mostly in the late 1970s. Some such groups use various editions of Anglican missals, which are principally the 1928 BCP with the addition of the missing Catholic elements taken from different editions of the Tridentine missal. It is worth noting, and it is indeed most important to note that those jurisdictions, though typically claiming Catholicism in one form or another, often under the name of "Anglo-Catholicism," are rife with Protestants and Protestant influence. It is this prevelent Protestant influence that renders it not possible simply to claim that the 1928 BCP is inherently Catholic in nature simply because Continuing Anglican tend to use it. Furthermore, it is known that there was much Protestant influence in the compilation of the 1928 BCP, as captured and summarized within the Articles of Religion, which we consider a shame due to the many beautiful elements the book otherwise possesses.

Within the Anglican Rite Roman Catholic Church, the 1928 BCP is not the standard of liturgy. The standard of liturgy is found within the Missale Anglicanum Editio Latina et Anglica and the Anglican Breviary. The aforementioned missal is not the 1928 BCP with certain elements added from Roman liturgy, but rather is essentially the pre-1955 Tridentine mass with certain acceptable elements added from the 1928 BCP, viz., the Collect for Purity, the Summary of the Law, the General Confession, Absolution, and Comfortable Words, and the General Thanksgiving after Communion. Indeed, our Particular Church is not a Continuing Anglican community, but rather an Old Roman Catholic Patriarchate that has, through her special history, inherited the blessing of Anglican heritage. It is important that our liturgy represent out heritage and, above all, the true Catholic doctrine, for *lex orandi lex credendi.*

While Can. 68 Sec. 1 of the Code of Particular Canon Law permits the use of certain other traditional Anglican and Roman liturgy, this is not intended to be the norm or standard use. It is never intended that there should be within our jurisdiction some parishes that use the official missal of our Patriarchate, other parishes that use different missals, and still other parishes that use the 1928 BCP. Such a mismatched collection of liturgy across parishes acts against the unity so essential to our mission. Yet, certain other liturgy may be, under Canon Law and with proper permission, use on occasion. Can. 68 Sec. 2 specifically addresses the issues pertaining to the effects of the Protestant Reformation on the 1928 BCP and earlier Books of Common Prayer. These effects cannot be ignored by anyone professing the Catholic Faith.

Can. 68 Sec. 3 specifically states that no liturgy may be used if said liturgy is used with intent to deny Catholic doctrine. This may further reasonably be interpreted to imply any liturgy which is inherently non-Catholic, regardless of the intent of the officiant and participant. In a valid sacrament there must be valid intent in accordance with Catholic doctrine on the part of the one performing the sacrament. The rite used is an external form, by the action of which the intent of the one performing the sacrament is realized and the grace of the said sacrament is conveyed. Therefore, it is illogical that a rite devoid of Catholic form could or should be used to convey a valid Catholic sacrament with the intent of actually conveying a valid Catholic sacrament. Due to the Protestant influence on the 1928 BCP, there is definite cause for concern as to whether it may be used in its unaltered and unedited form for the adminsitration of valid Catholic sacraments.

First, let us note that the current rites for ordination to the Minor Holy Orders under the *Pontificale Anglicanum* 3rd Ed. are derived from the ordination rites contained within the 1928 BCP, in order to provide stylistic influence from our Anglican heritage. These rites, though, are modified in order to be sufficient in form and intent for the administration of a valid Catholic sacrament. Furthermore, the 1928 BCP rites of marriage, visitation of the sick, and burial (outside a Requiem mass) are similarly found in our Rituale Anglicanum, again modified where needed to render them of a form appropriate to the admission of a valid Catholic sacrament. Such was and is the similar practice of the Anglican Use and the Anglican Ordinariate of the Roman Communion, i.e., that Anglican-style liturgy may be used, having been properly and sufficiently modified to be in accord with Catholic doctrine and tradition.

The chief concern pertaining to the use of the 1928 BCP regards its use for the administration of Holy Communion. Used in its unaltered form without any additions or deletions, it lacks many essential Catholic elements in the Sacrament. These may be briefly enumerated as follows:

1. There are no Prayers at the Foot of the Altar at the beginning of the communion service. This removes the act of the priest, servers, and people preparing themselves for the Holy Sacrifice. This also promotes Luther's refusal to accept the Catholic teaching that the priest is judge, witness and intercessor with God.

2. There is only a minimal calendar of Saints, consisting essentially only of the Apostles. Hence, there are also no collects of commemoration. Coupled with the statements made in the Articles of Religion, this can only be taken to be a denial of the Catholic doctrine pertaining to the Saints. That they are not included in the 1928 BCP renders it impossible to keep the Catholic feasts of the Saints. The various editions of Anglo-Catholic missals have had to remedy this chiefly through the addition of Roman Catholic collects.

3. There is no true Offertory. The priest merely "sets the table" for communion rather than formally offering the host and chalice. Without suitable words in the ritual by which the bread and wine are offered, the door is left wide open for any interpretation of the elements of communion, including that they do not become the very and true Body and Blood of Christ, but merely are representative and constitute a memorial meal. Even though the words "And the Priest shall then offer, and shall place upon the Holy Table, the Bread and the Wine" appear in the rubrics, this is far from sufficient to indicate the sacrificial nature of a true Holy Communion. The non-sacrificial interpretations that are clearly possible on the part of the priest and the people are entirely Protestant in nature and not consistent with Catholic doctrine.

4. In the Prayer for the Whole State of Christ's Church, the phrase "We humbly beseech thee most mercifully to accept our [alms and] oblations" appears, without any further

comment that would suggest a sacrificial nature. Indeed, that the oblations of bread and wine are written next to alms further weakens any possibility that the oblation of bread and wine in the 1928 BCP rite is necessarily and un-ambiguously a sacrificial offering to which the people may join themselves.

5. The 1928 BCP communion service lacks Secrets, by which the priest offers special prayers silently on behalf of the people. The lack of these prayers weakens the role of the priest in the sense of a Catholic priesthood, i.e., an alter Christus.

6. Most troubling is the prayer of consecration itself. The prayer refers to the Sacrifice of Christ on the Cross at Cal-vary. Instead of then referring to the present act on the altar as that same, true and living Sacrifice to which the priest and people join themselves, it explictly refers to the present act as a "perpetual memory" of the Sacrifice of Christ on the Cross. If it is the intent of the priest that communion be merely a memorial, then it is indeed no sac-rament at all.

7. While the phrase in the Invocation "...in remembrance of his death and passion, may be partakers of his most blessed Body and Blood" does refer to the Body and Blood of Christ and may otherwise not be a troubling statement, taken in the context in which the 1928 prayer of consecra-tion is phrased renders the statement in the Invocation merely the furtherance of the Protestant heresy that Holy Communion is merely a memorial. Further in the Invoca-tion is stated "And here we offer and present unto thee, O Lord, our selves, our souls and bodies, to be a reasonable, holy, and living sacrifice unto thee." This statement merely by itself represents Catholic doctrine. Yet, in the context of the entire rite, it becomes highly confusing as to the true nature of the communion service, i.e., is it a Sacrifice (Catholic doctrine) or merely a memorial (Protestant here-sy).

8. The *Agnus Dei* is completely missing.

9. There is no invocation of Saints, and there are no prayers for the dead, furthering the various Protestant heresies regarding the Saints and intercession for the dead.

10. There is no *Domine non sum dignus* per se, but there is the following prayer: "We do not presume to come to this thy Table, O merciful Lord, trusting in our own righteousness, but in thy manifold and great mercies. We are not worthy so much as to gather up the crumbs under thy Table. But thou art the same Lord, whose property is always to have mercy: Grant us therefore, gracious Lord, so to eat the flesh of thy dear Son Jesus Christ, and to drink his blood, that our sinful bodies may be made clean by his body, and our souls washed through his most precious blood, and that we may evermore dwell in him, and he in us. Amen." This prayer further adds to the confusion regarding the sacrificial nature of a true mass. Given the earlier aspects of the 1928 rite that suggest communion is not a sacrifice, but a memorial, this prayer furthers both that notion and the idea that the presence of Christ is mystical. That is, a denial of transubstantian, and hence of Catholic doctrine. Indeed, Article 28 of the Articles of Religion explicitly denies transubstantiation. Hence, all statements in the 1928 rite referring to the Body and Blood of Christ must be interpretted merely in a symbolic fashion. Thus, taken in its unaltered and unedited form, the rite of the 1928 BCP is not a true sacrifice.

11. The priest in the 1928 BCP rite does not keep his thumbs and forefingers joined until the ablutions. This action is done in traditional liturgy to prevent profanement of any particles of the Body of Christ that may be on the priests thumbs and forefingers. Furthermore, there is no explicit act of ablutions of the sacred vessels. That these actions are absent in the 1928 BCP rite is rather telling and certainly consistent with Article 28 of the Articles of Religion.

12. The Articles of Religion themselves, under which the intent of the 1928 BCP rites must be interpreted and considered, contain numerous anti-Catholic doctrine. This leads to the serious question of valid intent on the part of

anyone celebrating Holy Communion under the 1928 BCP rite.

It is, therefore, not permitted for any priest in the Anglican Rite Roman Catholic Church to celebrate the Holy Mass under the 1928 BCP without the permission of the Patriarch, in accordance with Can. 68 Sec. 1, and then only if the rite is celebrated under the following conditions:

1. It is celebrated out of an altar service book not containing the 39 Articles of Religion.

2. A nine-fold *Kyrie Eleison* is used.

3. The *Gloria in excelsis*, when liturgically required, is said after the Kyrie.

4. The Prayers at the Foot of the Altar are said as given in the *Missale Anglicanum*.

5. The Offertory must be said in accordance with the *Missale Anglicanum*.

6. The Canon of the Mass is said in its entirety as given in the *Missale Anglicanum*.

7. The intent must be in accordance with Catholic doctrine as delivered through Sacred Scripture and Sacred Tradition, which same is also promulgated through the Catechism of this Particular Church.

8. It must not otherwise violate rubrics and liturgical norms and instructions.

Given this day at the Court of Saint Mary of Walsingham, 15 July, in the year of our Lord 2012.

62 Theses Demonstrating Why The Preservation and Practice of the Traditional Latin Mass is Superior in Every Way to the Novus Ordo Missae

Edited by Keith Cardinal Steinhurst v.u.z. Westphalia

The Novus Ordo Missa is deficient because:

1. The New Mass is not an unequivocal Profession of the Catholic Faith. Unlike the traditional Latin Mass it is am-

biguous and Protestant. Therefore, since we pray as we believe (lex orandi lex credendi) it follows that we cannot pray with the New Mass in Protestant Fashion and still believe as a Catholic.

2. The changes [in the New Mass] were not just slight ones but actually "deal with a fundamental renovation ... a total change ... a new creation." (Msgr. A. Bugnini, co-author of the New Mass)

3. The New Mass leads us to think "that truths ... can be changed or ignored without infidelity to that sacred deposit of doctrine to which the Catholic Faith is bound forever." (Cardinals A. Ottaviani and A. Bacci to Pope Paul VI A Critical Study of the Novus Ordo Missae).

4. The New Mass represents "a striking departure from the Catholic theology of the Mass as formulated in Session XXII of the Council of Trent" which, in fixing the "canons," provided an "insurmountable barrier to any heresy against the integrity of the Mystery." (Cardinals A. Ottaviani and A. Bacci to Pope Paul VI A Critical Study of the Novus Ordo Missae).

5. The difference between the two is not simply one of mere detail or just modification of ceremony, but "all that is of perennial value finds only a minor place (in the New Mass), if it subsists at all." (Cardinals A. Ottaviani and A. Bacci to Pope Paul VI A Critical Study of the Novus Ordo Missae).

6. "Recent reforms have amply demonstrated that fresh changes in the liturgy could lead to nothing but complete bewilderment in the faithful who already show signs of uneasiness and lessening of Faith." (Cardinals A. Ottaviani and A. Bacci to Pope Paul VI A Critical Study of the Novus Ordo Missae).

7. In times of confusion such as now, we are guided by the words of our Lord: "By their fruits you shall know them." Fruits of the New Mass are: 30% decrease in Sunday Mass attendance in U.S. (NY Times 5/24/75), 43% decrease in France (Cardinal Marty), 50% decrease in Holland (NY Times 1/5/76).

8. "Amongst the best of the clergy the practical result (of the New Mass) is an agonizing crisis of conscience..." (Cardinals A. Ottaviani and A. Bacci to Pope Paul VI A Critical Study of the Novus Ordo Missae).

9. In less than seven years after the introduction of the New Mass, priests in the world decreased from 413,438 to 243,307 -- almost 50%! (Holy See Statistics)

10. "The pastoral reasons adduced to support such a grave break with tradition ... do not seem to us sufficient." (Cardinals A. Ottaviani and A. Bacci to Pope Paul VI A Critical Study of the Novus Ordo Missae).

11. The New Mass does not manifest Faith in the Real Presence of our Lord -- the Traditional Mass manifests it unmistakably.

12. The New Mass confuses the REAL Presence of Christ in the Eucharist with His MYSTICAL Presence among us (Protestant doctrine).

13. The New Mass blurs what ought to be a sharp difference between the HIERARCHIC Priesthood and the common priesthood of the people (Protestant doctrine).

14. The New Mass favors the heretical theory that it is THE FAITH of the people and not THE WORDS OF THE PRIEST that makes Christ present in the Eucharist.

15. The insertion of the Lutheran: "Prayer of the Faithful" in the New Mass follows and puts forth the Protestant error that all the people are priests.

16. The New Mass does away with the Confiteor of the priest, makes it collective with the people, thus promoting Luther's refusal to accept the Catholic teaching that the priest is judge, witness and intercessor with God.

17. The New Mass gives us to understand that the people concelebrate with the priest -- which is against Catholic theology!

18. Six Protestant ministers collaborated in making up the New Mass: George, Jasper, Shepherd, Kunneth, Smith and Thurian.

19. Just as Luther did away with the Offertory -- since it very clearly expressed the sacrificial, propitiatory character of the Mass -- so also the inventors of the New Mass did away with it, reducing it to a simple Preparation of the Gifts.

20. Enough Catholic theology has been removed that Protestants can, while keeping their antipathy for the True Roman Catholic Church, use the text of the New Mass without difficulty. Protestant Minister Thurian (co-consulter for the 'New Mass' project) said that a fruit of the New Mass "will perhaps be that the non-Catholic communities will be able to celebrate the Lord's Supper using the same prayers as the Catholic Church." (La Croix 4/30/69)

21. The narrative manner of the Consecration in the New Mass infers that it is only a memorial and not a true sacrifice (Protestant doctrine)

22. By grave omissions, the New Mass leads us to believe that it is only a meal (Protestant doctrine) and not a sacrifice for the remission of sins (Catholic Doctrine).

23. The changes such as: table instead of altar; facing people instead of tabernacle; Communion in the hand, etc., emphasize Protestant doctrines (e.g., Mass is only a meal; priest only a president of the assembly; Eucharist is NOT the Body, Blood, Soul and Divinity of Jesus Christ, but merely a piece of bread, etc.)

24. Protestants themselves have said, "the new Catholic Eucharistic prayers have abandoned the false (sic) perspective of sacrifice offered to God." (La Croix 12/10/69)

25. We are faced with the dilemma: either we become Protestant by worshipping with the New Mass, or else we preserve our Catholic Faith by adhering faithfully to the traditional Mass, the "Mass of All Time."

26. The New Mass was made in accordance with the Protestant definition of the Mass: "The Lord's Supper or Mass is a sacred assembly of the people of God which gathers together under the leadership of the priest to celebrate the memorial of the Lord." (Par. 7 Intro. to the New Missal, defining the New Mass, 4/6/69)

27. By means of ambiguity, the New Mass pretends to please Catholics while pleasing Protestants; thus it is "double-tongued" and offensive to God who abhors any kind of hypocrisy: "Cursed be ... the double-tongued for they destroy the peace of many." (Sirach 28:13)

28. Beautiful, familiar Catholic hymns which have inspired people for centuries, have been thrown out and replaced with new hymns strongly Protestant in sentiment, further deepening the already distinct impression that one is no longer attending a Catholic function.

29. The New Mass contains ambiguities subtly favoring heresy, which is more dangerous than if it were clearly heretical since a half-heresy half resembles the Truth!

30. Christ has only one Spouse, the Catholic Church, and her worship service cannot also serve religions that are at enmity with her.

31. The New Mass follows the format of Cranmer's heretical Anglican Mass, and the methods used to promote it follow precisely the methods of the English heretics.

32. Holy Mother Church canonized numerous English Martyrs who were killed because they refused to participate in a Mass such as the New Mass!

33. Protestants who once converted to Catholicism are scandalized to see that the New Mass is the same as the one they attended as Protestants. One of them, Julien Green, asks: "Why did we convert?"

34. Statistics show a great decrease in conversions to Catholicism following the use of the New Mass. Conversions, which were up to 100,000 a year in the U.S., have decreased to less than 10,000! And the number of people leaving the Church far exceeds those coming in.

35. The Traditional Mass has forged many saints. "Innumerable saints have been fed abundantly with the proper piety towards God by it ..." (Pope Paul VI, Const. Apost. Missale Romanum)

36. The nature of the New Mass is such as to facilitate profanations of the Holy Eucharist, which occur with a frequency unheard of with the Traditional Mass.

37. The New Mass, despite appearances, conveys a New Faith, not the Catholic Faith. It conveys Modernism and follows exactly the tactics of Modernism, using vague terminology in order to insinuate and advance error.

38. By introducing optional variations, the New Mass undermines the unity of the liturgy, with each priest liable to deviate as he fancies under the guise of creativity. Disorder inevitably results, accompanied by lack of respect and irreverence.

39. Many good Catholic theologians, canonists and priests do not accept the New Mass, and affirm that they are unable to celebrate it in good conscience.

40. The New Mass has eliminated such things as: genuflections (only three remain), purification of the priests fingers in the chalice, preservation from all profane contact of priest's fingers after Consecration, sacred altar stone and relics, three altar clothes (reduced to one), all of which "only serve to emphasize how outrageously faith in the dogma of the Real Presence is implicitly repudiated." (Cardinals A. Ottaviani and A. Bacci to Pope Paul VI A Critical Study of the Novus Ordo Missae).

41. The traditional Mass, enriched and matured by centuries of Sacred Tradition, was codified (not invented) by a Pope who was a saint, Pius V; whereas the New Mass was artificially fabricated by six Protestant ministers and a 33rd degree Freemason, i.e., Msgr. A Bugnini who was later exiled from the Vatican because of his ties with Freemasonry.

42. The errors of the New Mass, which are accentuated in the vernacular version, are even present in the Latin text of the New Mass.

43. The New Mass, with its ambiguity and permissiveness, exposes us to the wrath of God by facilitating the risk of invalid consecrations: "Will priests of the near future who have not received the traditional formation, and who rely

on the Novus Ordo Missae with the intention of 'doing what the Church does,' consecrate validly? One may be allowed to doubt it!" (Cardinals A. Ottaviani and A. Bacci to Pope Paul VI A Critical Study of the Novus Ordo Missae).

44. The abolition of the Traditional Mass recalls the prophecy of Daniel 8:12: "And he was given power against the perpetual sacrifice because of the sins of the people" and the observation of St. Alphonsus de Liguori that because the Mass is the best and most beautiful thing which exists in the Church here below, the devil has always tried by means of heretics to deprive us of it.

45. In places where the Traditional Mass is preserved, the Faith and fervor of the people are greater. Whereas the opposite is true where the New Mass reigns (Report on the Mass, Diocese of Campos, ROMA, Buenos Aires #69, 8/81)

46. Along with the New Mass goes also a new catechism, a new morality, new prayers, new Code of Canon law, new calendar, -- in a word, a NEW CHURCH, a complete revolution from the old. "The liturgical reform ... do not be deceived, this is where the revolution begins." (Msgr. Dwyer, Archbishop of Birmingham, spokesman of Episcopal Synod)

47. The intrinsic beauty of the Traditional Mass attracts souls by itself; whereas the New Mass, lacking any attractiveness of its own, has to invent novelties and entertainments in order to appeal to the people.

48. The New mass embodies numerous errors condemned by Pope St. Pius V at the Council of Trent (Mass totally in vernacular, words of Consecration spoken aloud, etc. See Condemnation of Jansenist Synod of Pistia), and errors condemned by Pope Pius XII (e.g., altar in form of table. See Mediator Dei).

49. The New Mass attempts to transform the Catholic Church into a new, ecumenical church embracing all ideologies and all religions -- right and wrong, truth and error -- a goal long dreamt of by the enemies of the Catholic Church.

50. The New Mass, in removing the salutations and final blessing when the priest celebrates alone, shows a denial of, and disbelief in the dogma of the Communion of Saints.

51. The altar and tabernacle are now separated, thus marking a division between Christ in His priest-and-Sacrifice-on-the-altar, from Christ in His Real Presence in the tabernacle, "two things which of their very nature, must remain together." (Pius XII)

52. The New Mass no longer constitutes a vertical worship between God and man, but rather a horizontal worship between man and man.

53. The New Mass, although appearing to conform to the dispositions of Vatican Council II, in reality opposes its instructions, since the Council itself declared its desire to conserve and promote the Traditional Rite.

54. The Traditional Latin Mass of Pope St. Pius V has never been legally abrogated and therefore remains a true rite of the Roman Catholic Church by which the faithful may fulfill their Sunday obligation.

55. Pope St. Pius V granted a perpetual indult, valid "for always," to celebrate the Traditional Mass freely, licitly, without scruple of conscience, punishment, sentence or censure (Papal Bull "Quo Primum")

56. Pope Paul VI, when promulgating the New Mass, himself declared. "The rite ... by itself is NOT a dogmatic definition ..." (11/19/69)

57. Pope Paul VI, when asked by Cardinal Heenan of England, if he was abrogating or prohibiting the Tridentine Mass, answered: "It is not our intention to prohibit absolutely the Tridentine Mass."

58. Because "In the Libera Nos of the New Mass, the Blessed Virgin, the Apostles and all the Saints are no longer mentioned; her and their intercession thus no longer asked, even in time of peril." (Cardinals A. Ottaviani and A. Bacci to Pope Paul VI A Critical Study of the Novus Ordo Missae).

59. In none of the tree new Eucharistic Prayers (of the New Mass) is there any reference ... to the state of suffering of those who have died, in none the possibility of a particular Memento, thus undermining faith in the redemptive nature of the Sacrifice. (Cardinals A. Ottaviani and A. Bacci to Pope Paul VI A Critical Study of the Novus Ordo Missae).

60. We recognize the Holy Father's supreme authority in his universal government of Holy Mother Church, but we know that even this authority cannot impose upon us a practice which is so CLEARLY against the Faith: a Mass that is equivocal and favoring heresy and therefore disagreeable to God.

61. As stated in Vatican Council I, the "Holy Spirit was not promised to the successors of Peter, that by His revelation they might make new doctrine, but that by His assistance they might inviolably keep and faithfully expound the revelation or deposit of Faith delivered through the Apostles." (Dnz 3070)

62. Heresy, or whatever clearly favors heresy, cannot be a matter for obedience. Obedience is at the service of Faith and not Faith at the service of obedience! In this foregoing case then, "One must obey God before men." (Acts 5:29)

Placing of Jesu Bambino
on the Eve of the Nativity
Caeremoniale ASMW 2015 LVI

This rite takes places on the Eve of Christmas, either immediately before the First Mass of Christmas, or sometime earlier, but always after I Vespers of Christmas. The figure of Gesu Bambino is placed on a cushion. The procession forms just as the procession would form for mass. The Celebrant is vested in alb, cope, and biretta (or optionally in surplice, cope, and biretta if the ceremony takes place earlier). The Sacred Ministers of the mass process immediately before the Celebrant if they are in mass vestments, regardless of the time of the ceremony.

Suitable hymns of Christmas may be sung as the procession takes place. Those in the procession go to their places as usual, and the Celebrant takes the figure of Gesu Bambino to the praesepio (crib), which should be set up in some suitable location. It may be as part of a larger Nativity scene, or it may be a stand-alone praesepio, or it may be a permanent fixture on the altar. This varies by parish. But note that a temporary praesepio should not be placed on the altar. If it is to be on the altar, it should be of a design for this purpose, e.g., above the tabernacle.

The Celebrant remains standing and places the figure of Gesu Bambino in the praesepio. Once the Celebrant has placed the figure, the Celebrant gives up his biretta to a server. The thurifer brings the thurible, and the Celebrant blesses incense as usual. The Celebrant then censes, standing, the figure with three double-swings. Returning the thurible to the thurifer, the Celebrant then kneels and kisses the foot of Gesu Bambino. He then takes the biretta. The other Sacred Ministers, if they are in mass vestments, then proceed to do likewise (otherwise they take their place in line with the choir). Next, the clergy in choir process forward to kiss the foot of Gesu Bambino. The servers follow.

Then the faithful may be invited forward. They kneel at the communion rail. The Celebrant takes the figure of Gesu Bambino from the praesepio as the faithful come forward and takes it singly around to each of them to kiss. This having been completed, the Celebrant returns Gesu Bambino to the praesepio.

If the officiant at this ritual is a Bishop, then he vests either in alb, cope, and mitre or rochet, cope, and mitre. If this ritual takes place immediately before mass, then it should occur at the end of Matins, being the Office immediately preceding the Midnight Mass.

The procession forms as for a pontifical mass. The Assistant Deacons, if any, should be in dalmatics, and the Assistant Priest should be vested in a cope. All proceeds as described above. The Bishop, standing with the mitre, places Gesu Bambino in the praesepio. He then gives up the mitre to the Assistant Deacon, who hands it to the Mitre Bearer. The thurifer brings the thurible, and the Bishop censes the figure as described above. The Bishop then kneels and kisses the foot of the figure, and all else proceeds as above. The Bishop sits with the mitre at the throne or faldstool while the clergy and servers reverence Gesu Bambino. He stands, wearing the mitre, and takes the figure to bring it to the people at the communion rail.

Marking of Houses
on the Feast of the Epiphany
Caeremoniale ASMW 2015 LVII

On the Feast of the Epiphany or during the Octave thereof, the priest may go to the houses of the faithful and bless them with the Epiphany Water that was made on the Eve of the Epiphany. The house is blessed according to the *Rituale Anglicanum*, using Epiphany Water. Then the priest goes to the outside of the main door of the house and marks it with chalk that had likewise been blessed on the Eve of the Epiphany. The markings consist of the first two digits of the year and the initials of the three Kings, Caspar, Melchior, and Balthazar, all separated by crosses, and the final two digits of the year. The marking is made as follows:

$$20 + C + M + B + 22$$

Bells and the Elevations During Papal Masses

The following applies to all papal masses,
regardless of solemnity.

1. The altar bells are not rung at any point during papal masses.

2. At the elevation of the Host, the archfather elevates the host as usual. Then at the height of the elevation, he makes a semi-circle, turning first to the Epistle side, then to the Gospel side, and then returning to the centre.

3. The same semi-circle is repeated for the elevation of the Chalice.

NOVEMBER & DECEMBER

ADVENT AND CHRISTMAS

ಐಂಡಿ

General Notes on Advent

The Colour of the Day is purple throughout Advent. Feasts are in their proper colour. For Gaudete Sunday and all ferial days thereafter (excluding the Ember Days), the Colour of the Day may be rose in place of purple, but purple remains appropriate. Purple must be used for the liturgy of the season during the three Ember Days. Purple is also the colour for the Vigil of the Nativity, and white is only used beginning with the first mass of the Feast of the Nativity.

The altar and church in general should be decorated modestly, due to the penitential and preparatory nature of Advent. Altar flowers are permitted, but should be modest. The *Gloria* is not said throughout the season except on feasts. The regular dismissal, *Ite Missa Est* or *Depart in Peace*, is replaced by *Benedicamus Domino* or *Let us bless the Lord* in all masses of the season, but not of feasts. The Preface of the Most Holy Trinity is said on Sundays, and the Common Preface is used at ferial masses and masses of feasts on weekdays, except when another preface is specified in the rubrics.

An advent wreath may be used, placed on either side of the altar, consisting of four purple candles and a white candle in the center, or three purple candles, one rose candle, and a central white candle. They may be decorated with holly and other appropriate, yet modest decoration. The appropriate candles are lit after the altar candles are lit, but before the mass begins.

Only feasts of the rank of Semi-double and higher or votive masses of third class or higher may be celebrated as the principal mass on ferial days of Advent. Only First Class votive masses may be celebrated as the principle mass on Sundays during Advent, except the First Sunday during Advent, during which time votive masses may not be celebrated as the principle mass.

Feasts celebrated during Advent require that the feria be commemorated. If a ferial mass is said, and there is a simple feast appointed for the same day, then the simple feast may be commemorated at the ferial mass.

For Feasts of simple rank and votive masses of the 4th class, they may be celebrated, but not as the principal mass, or when specifically prohibited by the rubrics. In these cases, the feria should also be commemorated. The votive mass for solemnization of Holy Matrimony is not used during Advent.

At feasts during Advent, the Advent Feria is commemorated by saying the collect for the Sunday preceding it. This commemoration goes before the Seasonal Collects and other commemorations under one ending with them.

In the Divine Offices, the *Te Deum* is not said except in offices of feasts of semi-double or higher rank. The Dominical Preces are said at Prime and Compline on Sundays during Advent unless the Immaculate Conception or a Votive Mass of the First Class falls on a Sunday. Dominical Preces are also used at feasts during Advent of semi-double rank. The Preces are said kneeling at all office of the Advent feriae, and for those days, also the Psalms of Lauds 2 are used. Also, the Suffrage of All Saints is omitted, even on feasts.

✤ **28 NOVEMBER – SUNDAY – sɪ., sd., p.**

FIRST SUNDAY IN ADVENT

29 NOVEMBER – MONDAY – gnfp., p.
Feria II after Advent I (gnpf., p.)
Comm: Saint Saturninus, M. (s., r.)

30 NOVEMBER – TUESDAY – dɪ, r.

SAINT ANDREW THE APOSTLE
Saint Bibiana, Virgin & Martyr
Comm: Feria III after Advent I (gnpf., p.)

1 **December** – **Wednesday** – d., w.
Saint Leo X, Pope & Confessor
Comm: Feria IV after Advent I (gnpf., p.)
The mass is Si Diliges Me.

2 **December** – **Thursday** – sd., r.
Saint Bibiana, Virgin & Martyr
Comm: Feria V after Advent I (gnpf., p.)

3 **December** – **Friday** – gd., w.
Saint Francis Xavier, Confessor
Comm: Feria VI after Advent I (gnpf., p.)

4 **December** – **Saturday** – d., w.
Saint Peter Chrysologus
Bishop, Confessor, & Doctor of the Church
Comm: Saturday after Advent I (gnpf., p.)
and Saint Barbara, V.M. (r.)

✚ 5 **December** – **Sunday** – s2., sd., p.

Second Sunday in Advent
Comm: St. Sabbas, Ab. (w.)

6 **December** – **Monday** – d., w.
Saint Nicholas, Bishop & Confessor
Comm: Feria II after Advent II (gnpf., p.)

7 **December** – **Tuesday** – d., w.
Saint Ambrose,
Bishop, Confessor, & Doctor of the Church
Comm: Feria III after Advent II (gnpf., p.) and the Vigil of
the Immaculate Conception of the BVM (min. vig., p.)

N.b. Nothing is said of the vigil in the Offices.

*N.b. At Vespers begins the Office of the
Immaculate Conception.*

✚ **8 December – Wednesday** – d1 with oct.3, w./mb.

Immaculate Conception
of the Blessed Virgin Mary

Comm: Feria IV after Advent II (gnpf., p.)

✝ **FESTAL STATION AT THE BASILICA OF ST. MARK, VENICE** ✝

FEAST DAY OF THE ORDER OF THE EAGLE
OF ST. STEPHEN AND MARY IMMACULATE

*N.b. The Preface for the Immaculate Conception is used at
all masses not of the season during the Octave,
unless another be appointed.*

9 December – Thursday – sd., w.
Saint Pius IV, Pope & Confessor
*Comm: Of the Oct. of the Immaculate Conception of the
BVM (oct.3, w./mb.) and Feria V after Advent II (gnpf., p.)*

The mass is Si Diliges Me.

10 December – Friday – oct.3, w./mb.
Of the Oct. of the Immaculate Conception of the BVM
*Comm: Feria VI after Advent II (gnpf., p.) and
Saint Melichiades, P.M. (s., r.)*

11 December – Saturday – sd., w.

Saint Damasus I, Pope & Confessor
*Comm: Octave of the Immaculate Conception (oct.3, w./mb.)
and Saturday after Advent II (gnpf., p.)*

✚ **12 December – Sunday** – s2., sd., rs./p.

Third Sunday in Advent
ALSO KNOWN AS

GAUDETE SUNDAY
Comm: Of the Oct. of the Immaculate Conception of the BVM (oct.3, w./mb.)

13 DECEMBER – MONDAY – d., r.
Saint Lucy, Virgin and Martyr
*Comm: Octave of the Immaculate Conception
(oct.3, w./mb.) and Feria II after Advent III (gnpf., rs./p.)*

14 DECEMBER – TUESDAY – oct.3, w./mb.
Of the Oct. of the Immaculate Conception of the BVM
Comm: Feria III after Advent III (gnpf., rs./p.)

15 DECEMBER – WEDNESDAY – gd., w./mb.
*Octave Day of the Immaculate Conception
of the Blessed Virgin Mary*
Comm: Ember Wednesday of Advent (gnpf., p.)

16 DECEMBER – THURSDAY – sd., r.
Saint Eusebius, Bishop & Martyr
Comm: Feria V after Advent III (gnpf., rs./p.)

17 DECEMBER – FRIDAY – gnpf., p.
Ember Friday of Advent

18 DECEMBER – SATURDAY – gnpf., p.
Ember Saturday of Advent

✠ **19 DECEMBER – SUNDAY** – s2., sd., p.
FOURTH SUNDAY IN ADVENT

20 DECEMBER – MONDAY – min. vig., p.
Vigil of Saint Thomas the Apostle
Comm: Feria II after Advent IV (gnpf., p.)

N.b. Nothing is said of the vigil in the Offices.

21 DECEMBER – TUESDAY – d2./r.

SAINT THOMAS, APOSTLE

Comm: Feria III after Advent IV (gnpf., p.)

22 DECEMBER – WEDNESDAY – gnpf., p.
Feria IV after Advent IV

23 DECEMBER – THURSDAY – gnpf., p.
Feria V after Advent IV

24 DECEMBER – FRIDAY – d1/p.
Vigil of the Nativity of Our Lord

*The colour remains purple until the First Mass of the Nativity.
Compline is sung as in the Advent season. The First Mass of
the Nativity should begin at the earliest such that the Canon
should being at midnight.*

*Preferrably the Ordinary of the Mass should not begin until mid-
night. However, should it be permitted for pastoral reasons by the
local Ordinary to begin at an earlier time, under no circumstances
shall it begin before Vespers is said.*

---

*The placing of Jesu Bambino takes place at some time after
I Vespers of the Nativity and before the First Mass thereof.
The Christmas Proclamation is sung as given in the
Ceremonial prior to the procession at the First Mass.*

✤ 25 DECEMBER – SATURDAY – d1./w.

FEAST OF THE NATIVITY OF OUR LORD JESUS CHRIST

FIRST MASS – *at Night*
SECOND MASS – *at Sunrise*
Commemoration at 2nd mass: Saint Anatasia
THIRD MASS – *during the Day*

N.b. A single priest celebrating all three masses (or two masses) of the Nativity should follow the procedures given in the rubrics for All Souls' Day.

✤ 26 DECEMBER – SUNDAY – d2/r.

SAINT STEPHEN DEACON AND PROTOMARTYR

PATRON OF THE ANGLICAN PATRIARCHATE
ANGLICAN RITE ROMAN CATHOLIC CHURCH
Comm: Sunday within the Octave of the Nativity (sd., w.)

+ FESTAL STATION AT THE
BASILICA OF SAN STEFANO AL PONTE, FLORENCE +

27 DECEMBER – MONDAY – d2/r.

SAINT JOHN APOSTLE AND EVANGELIST

Comm: Octaves of the Nativity (sd., w.) and of Saint Stephen (r.)

28 DECEMBER – TUESDAY – d2./r.

HOLY INNOCENTS, MARTYRS

Comm: Octave of the Nativity (sd., w.), Octave of Saint Stephen (r.), and Octave of Saint John (r.)

29 DECEMBER – WEDNESDAY – d./r.
Saint Thomas, Bishop and Martyr
*Comm: Octave of Saint Stephen (r.), Octave of Saint John
(r.), and Octave of the Holy Innocents (r.)*

30 DECEMBER – THURSDAY – oct./w.
Within the Octave of the Nativity
*Comm: Octave of St. Stephen (sd., r.), Octave of Saint John
(r.), and Octave of the Holy Innocents (r.)*

31 DECEMBER – FRIDAY – d., w.
Saint Sylvester, Pope and Confessor
*Comm: Octave of the Nativity (sd., w.), Octave of
Saint John (w.), and Octave of the Holy Innocents (r.)*

JANUARY

CHRISTMAS, EPIPHANY, AND
THE CHRISTMAS CYCLE

The first of January is both the Octave Day of Christmas and the Feast of the Circumcision or the Feast of the Presentation of Our Lord Jesus Christ in the Temple. Christmastide continues until First Vespers of the Feast of the Epiphany on the sixth of January. The Christmas Cycle begins after Second Vespers of the Octave Day of the Epiphany (Baptism of Our Lord) and continues until None on Saturday before Septuagesima.

✤ 1 JANUARY – SATURDAY – d2, w.

PRESENTATION OF CHRIST
IN THE TEMPLE
OCTAVE DAY OF THE NATIVITY
*Comm: Octaves of Saint Stephen, Saint John,
and the Holy Innocents*

✤ 2 JANUARY – SUNDAY – d2., w.

Commemoration of the Most Holy Name of Jesus
*Comm: Octave Day of Saint Stephen,
Deacon & Protomartyr (gd., s., r.)*
**PATRON OF THE ANGLICAN PATRIARCHATE
ANGLICAN RITE ROMAN CATHOLIC CHURCH**
Comm: Octaves of Saint John and the Holy Innocents

3 JANUARY – MONDAY – gd., s., w.
Octave Day of Saint John, Apostle and Evangelist
Comm: Octave of the Holy Innocents

4 JANUARY – TUESDAY – gd., s., r.
Octave Day of the Holy Innocents

5 JANUARY – WEDNESDAY – maj. vig. 2, sd., w.

VIGIL OF THE EPIPHANY

Comm: Saint Telephorus, P.M. (r.)

*N.b. It is an ancient custom to perform the Blessing of
Water as appointed in the Rituale for this day.*

✚ 6 JANUARY – THURSDAY – d1 with priv. oct. 2, w.

MANIFESTATION OF CHRIST
TO THE GENTILES

ALSO KNOWN AS THE EPIPHANY

*N.b. It is an ancient custom to bless gold, frankincense, and
myrrh this day. The Marking of Houses may be done as
given in the Ceremonial (see Introduction).*

7 JANUARY – FRIDAY – oct. 2, w.
Of the Octave of the Epiphany

8 JANUARY – SATURDAY – oct. 2, w.
Of the Octave of the Epiphany

✚ 9 JANUARY – SUNDAY – gd., oct. 2, w.

Holy Family of Jesus, Mary, and Joseph
*Comm: Sunday within the Octave of the Epiphany
(oct. 2, w.)*

10 JANUARY – MONDAY – oct. 2, w.
Of the Octave of the Epiphany

11 JANUARY – TUESDAY – oct. 2, w.
Of the Octave of the Epiphany
Comm: Saint Hyginus, P.M. (s., r.)

12 January – Wednesday – oct. 2, w.
Of the Octave of the Epiphany

13 January – Thursday – oct. day 2, gd., w.

Octave Day of the Epiphany
and the Baptism of
Our Lord Jesus Christ

*N.b. Jesu Bambino is removed from the praesepio and
processed out after II Vespers this day.*

14 January – Friday – d., w.
Saint Hilary
Bishop, Confessor, & Doctor of the Church
Comm: Saint Felix, Pr.M. (s., r.)

15 January – Saturday – d., w.
Saint Paul the First Hermit, Confessor
Comm: Saint Maurus, Ab. (w.)

✤ 16 January – Sunday – sd., g.
Second Sunday after Epiphany
Comm: Saint Marcellus I, P.M. (sd., r.)

17 January – Monday – d., w.
Saint Anthony, Abbot

18 January – Tuesday – gd., w.
The Chair of Saint Peter in Rome
Comm: Of Saint Paul (as usual) and St. Prisca, V.M. (r.)

19 JANUARY – WEDNESDAY – s., r.
*Saints Marius, Martha, Audifax,
and Habakkuk, MM. (s., r.)*
Comm: Saint Canute, K.M. (r.)

20 JANUARY – THURSDAY – d., r.
*Saint Fabian, Pope and Martyr,
and Saint Sebastian, Martyr*

21 JANUARY – FRIDAY – d., r.
Saint Agnes, Virgin and Martyr

22 JANUARY – SATURDAY – sd., r.
Saints Vincent and Anastasius, Martyrs

✚ 23 JANUARY – SUNDAY – sd., g.
Third Sunday after Ephiphany
*Comm: Saint Raymond de Pennafort, C. (sd., w.)
and Saint Emerentiana, VM. (r.)*

24 JANUARY – MONDAY – d., r.
Saint Timothy, Bishop and Martyr

25 JANUARY – TUESDAY – gd., r.
Conversion of Saint Paul
Comm: Of Saint Peter (as usual)

26 JANUARY – WEDNESDAY – d., r.
Saint Polycarp, Bishop and Martyr

27 JANUARY – THURSDAY – d., w.
*Saint John Chrysostom
Bishop, Confessor, and Doctor of the Church*

28 JANUARY – FRIDAY – d., w.
Saint Peter Nolasco, Confessor
Comm: Saint Agnes, V.M. (2nd Mass, r.)

29 JANUARY – SATURDAY – d., w.
Saint Francis de Sales
Bishop, Confessor, & Doctor of the Church

✠ **30 JANUARY – SUNDAY** – sd., g.
Fourth Sunday after Epiphany
Comm: Saint Martina, V.M. (sd., r.)

31 JANUARY – MONDAY – d., w.
Comm: Saint John Bosco, C. (d., w.)

FEBRUARY
CHRISTMAS CYCLE & SEPTUAGESIMATIDE

In Septuagesimatide, *Alleluia* is removed from Masses and Offices of the Season. The *Te Deum* is also not said in the Offices of the Season. Psalms of Lauds 2 are used except where otherwise directed.

1 FEBRUARY – TUESDAY – d., r.
Saint Ignatius, Bishop and Martyr

2 FEBRUARY – WEDNESDAY – d2, p.→ w.
PURIFICATION OF THE BLESSED VIRGIN MARY

N.b. The blessing of candles and the procession as appointed take place this day.

3 FEBRUARY – THURSDAY – s., r.
Saint Blaise, Bishop & Martyr

N.b. The blessing of throats according to the Rituale is commonly done this day.

4 FEBRUARY – FRIDAY –d., w.
Saint Andrew Corsini, Bishop & Confessor

5 FEBRUARY – SATURDAY – d., r.
Saint Agatha, Virgin and Martyr

✚ 6 FEBRUARY – SUNDAY – d.,w.

Saint Titus, Bishop and Confessor
Comm: Epiphany V (sd., g.) and Saint Dorothy, V.M. (r.)

7 FEBRUARY – MONDAY – d., w.
Saint Pius IX, Pope & Confessor
Comm: Saint Romuald, Ab. (d., w.)

8 FEBRUARY – TUESDAY – d., w.
Saint John of Matha, Confessor

9 FEBRUARY – WEDNESDAY – d., w.
Saint Cyril of Alexandria,
Bishop, Confessor, & Doctor of the Church
Comm: Saint Apollonia, V.M. (r.)

10 FEBRUARY – THURSDAY – d., w.
Saint Scholastica, Virgin

11 FEBRUARY – FRIDAY – gd., w./mb.
The Apparition of the Blessed Virgin Mary

12 FEBRUARY – SATURDAY – d., w.
Seven Holy Founders of the Servite Order
Comm: Epiphany VI (sd., g.) transferred

N.b. The Epiphany VI mass has
all the privileges of a Sunday.

✚ 13 FEBRUARY – SUNDAY – s2, sd., p.

SEPTUAGESIMA

14 FEBRUARY – MONDAY – s., r.
Saint Valentine, Priest & Martyr

15 FEBRUARY – TUESDAY – s., r.
Saints Faustinus & Jovita, Martyrs

16 FEBRUARY – WEDNESDAY – f., p.
Feria IV after Septuagesima

17 FEBRUARY – THURSDAY – f., p.
Feria V after Septuagesima

18 FEBRUARY – FRIDAY – s., r.
Saint Simeon, Bishop & Martyr

*N.b. Vespers this day is of
the Saturday Office of Our Lady
with commemoration of the feast.*

19 FEBRUARY – SATURDAY – s., mb./w.
Saturday Mass of Our Lady

*N.b. The Office is the Saturday Office of Our
Lady through None*

✚ 20 FEBRUARY – SUNDAY – s2, sd., p.

SEXAGESIMA

21 FEBRUARY – MONDAY – d., w.
Saint Julius II, Pope & Confessor

N.b. The mass is Si diliges me.

22 FEBRUARY – TUESDAY – gd., w.
Chair of Saint Peter in Antioch

23 FEBRUARY – WEDNESDAY – d., w.
Saint Peter Damian,
Bishop, Confessor, & Doctor of the Church
Comm: Vigil of Saint Mathias, A.

24 FEBRUARY – THURSDAY – d2, r.
SAINT MATHIAS, APOSTLE

25 FEBRUARY – FRIDAY – f., p.
Feria VI after Sexagesima

N.b. Vespers this day is of
the Saturday Office of Our Lady.

26 FEBRUARY – SATURDAY – s., mb./w.
Saturday Mass of Our Lady
N.b. The Office is the Saturday Office of Our
Lady through None

✚ 27 FEBRUARY – SUNDAY – s2, sd., p.

QUINQUAGESIMA
Comm: Saint Gabriel of Our Lady of Sorrows (d., w.)

28 FEBRUARY – MONDAY – f., p.
Feria II after Quinquagesima

MARCH

LENT

ಬೂಡಿ

1 MARCH – TUESDAY – d., w.
Saint David, Bishop & Confessor
Comm: Feria II after Quinquagesima (f., p.)

2 MARCH – WEDNESDAY – gpf., p.

ASH WEDNESDAY

*N.b. No masses other than that of Ash Wednesday
are said this day.*

*N.b. If the Bishop will expulse public penitents from the
Church this day, it is done at a regular mass of Ash
Wednesday in the manner prescribed in the Pontificale.*

+ LENTEN STATION AT THE
THE MOST HOLY PATRIARCHAL BASILICA OF SANTA MARIA ANTIQUA +

During Lent, the color of the day is purple. If there is a feast, it is celebrated using its proper color. If a feast or votive mass is said during Lent on a ferial day, the feria is always commemorated under one ending with the collect of the feast before the seasonal collects and other commemorations, and the Last Gospel is the Gospel from the ferial mass appointed for that day. The Nuptial votive mass is not said in Lent, but is merely commemorated (see the rubrics). Ferial masses in Lent have appointed prayers over the people at the end. These are used only at the ferial masses, and not at feasts. The *Gloria in Excelsis* is not said at any mass except feasts during Lent. During Passiontide, the *Gloria Patri* is omitted from all Masses and Offices of the Season.

In Lent, the *Alleluia* continues to be removed from Masses and Offices of the Season. The *Te Deum* is not said in the Offices of the Season. Psalms of Lauds 2 are used except where otherwise directed. Ferial preces are used in

18

Offices of the Season beginning with Ash Wednesday and continuing through Passiontide except where noted.

Dominical Preces are said at Prime and Compline on Sundays during Lent. Preces are said kneeling at all ferial offices of the season.

Instruction regarding anticipation of Offices and Rites during Lent

1. The custom as given in the rubrics of the breviary of anticipating the Offices of Lent is to be the preferred usage. Matins and Lauds should be said the evening prior. Other offices are said in the morning hours, and Vespers is said prior to the principal meal of the day, which same is taken to be the midday meal. Compline should be said after Vespers and typically around mid-afternoon to sunset.

2. Mass of the Institution of the Lord's Supper on Maundy Thursday, the Maundy itself, and Vespers should all be said in the morning.

3. If the Holy Oils are to be blessed on Maundy Thursday, then they are blessed in the usual manner at the Solemn Mass of Holy Thursday, and the specific Chrism Mass is not used. If they are to be blessed on Monday or Tuesday of Holy Week, then the mass is the Chrism Mass as given in the missal, and the Chrism Mass on those days should be said in the afternoon or evening, with the morning mass being of the day of Holy Week.

4. If there are Public Penitents to be re-admitted to the Church on Holy Thursday, then it must be after Lauds of Holy Thursday. This rite may take place either with a votive mass for the Forgiveness of Sins on Wednesday evening following Lauds, or else immediately preceding the Mass of Holy Thursday.

5. The Solemn Liturgy of Good Friday is to be said likewise in the morning prior to Vespers of that day.

6. The Liturgy of Holy Saturday and the Easter Vigil should be said in the morning and followed by Vespers as given in the Second Edition of the Missale Anglicanum Editio Latina et Anglica.

Instruction Regarding Fasting, Abstinence, Penance, & Self-Denial During Lent
Taken from the Patriarchal Motu Proprio "Sacrifice is a Key"
18 September A.D. 2018

1. On Ash Wendesday, Good Friday, and all Fridays of Lent, an act of self-denial, sacrifice, and penance shall be undertaken by all clergy and faithful. This act is of the choosing of the individual, provided it meets the spirit and intent of penance lot that will do I have to hear I have to hear what you said it would not otherwise get an idea as will see. Acts of charity towards others have always been the primary form of giving of one's self in sacrifice and penance within this See.

2. The abstention from all flesh meat or of red meat, as well as fasting in its usual form, may, as a matter of tradition, be continued and undertaken as the act of self-denial, sacrifice, and penance, but is not required.

3. The Patriarchal See, as well as jurisdictional bishops and superiors of religious communities and orders may impose specific acts of penance as deemed appropriate.

The requirement of penance is lifted, as in current use, under the following conditions:

1. If a semi-double or greater feast falls on a Lenten Friday or Lenten Ember Day, excepting Good Friday, the requirement is lifted.

2. The clergy and faithful are not required to take the exemption and may undertake their penance as they would otherwise do.

3 MARCH – THURSDAY – gnpf., p.
Feria V after Ash Wednesday

4 MARCH – FRIDAY – sd., w.
Saint Casimir, Confessor
Comm: Feria VI after Ash Wednesday (gnpf., p.)
and Saint Lucius I, P.M. (r.)

5 MARCH – SATURDAY – gnpf., p.
Saturday after Ash Wednesday

+ LENTEN STATION AT THE
MOST HOLY PAPAL BASILICA OF ST. PETER +

✚ 6 MARCH – SUNDAY – SI., sd., p.

FIRST SUNDAY IN LENT

Comm: Saints Perpetua and Felicitas, MM. (d., r.)

7 MARCH – MONDAY – d., w.
Saint Thomas Aquinas,
Confessor & Doctor of the Church
Comm: Feria II after Lent I (gnpf., p.)

8 MARCH – TUESDAY – d., w.
Saint John of God, Confessor
Comm: Feria III after Lent I (gnpf., p.)

9 MARCH – WEDNESDAY – d., w.
Saint Francis of Rome, Widow
Comm: Ember Wednesday in Lent (gnpf., p.)

+ LENTEN STATION AT THE
MOST HOLY PATRIARCHAL BASILICA OF SAN STEFANO AL PONTE +

10 MARCH – THURSDAY – sd., r.
Forty Holy Martyrs
Comm: Feria V after Lent I (gnpf., p.)

11 MARCH – FRIDAY – gnpf., p.
Ember Friday in Lent

12 **MARCH** – **SATURDAY** – d., w.
Saint Gregory the Great
Pope, Confessor, & Doctor of the Church
Comm: Ember Saturday in Lent (gnpf., p.)

✚ LENTEN STATION AT THE
CATHEDRAL OF SANTA MARIA DEL FIORE, FLORENCE ✚

✚ 13 **MARCH** – **SUNDAY** – SI., sd., p.

SECOND SUNDAY IN LENT

14 **MARCH** – **MONDAY** – gnpf., p.
Feria II after Lent II

15 **MARCH** – **TUESDAY** – gnpf., p.
Feria III after Lent II

16 **MARCH** – **WEDNESDAY** – gnpf., p.
Feria IV after Lent II

✚ LENTEN STATION AT THE
CATHEDRAL OF SAINT STEPHEN & SANTA MARIA ASSUNTA, PAVIA ✚

17 **MARCH** – **THURSDAY** – d., w.
Saint Patrick, Bishop & Confessor
Comm: Feria V after Lent II (gnpf., p.)

FEAST DAY OF THE ORDER OF THE EAGLE
OF ST. STEPHEN AND MARY IMMACULATE

18 **MARCH** – **FRIDAY** – d., w.
Saint Cyril of Jerusalem
Bishop, Confessor, & Doctor of the Church
Comm: Feria VI after Lent II (gnpf., p.)

19 MARCH – SATURDAY – dı, w.

SAINT JOSEPH
SPOUSE OF THE
BLESSED VIRGIN MARY AND
UNIVERSAL PATRON OF THE CHURCH

Comm: Saturday after Lent II (gnpf., p.)

+ LENTEN STATION AT THE
BASILICA OF SAINT MARK, VENICE +

✚ 20 MARCH – SUNDAY – SI., sd., p.

THIRD SUNDAY IN LENT

Comm: Saint Cuthbert, B.C. (d., w.)

21 MARCH – MONDAY – gd., w.
Saint Benedict, Abbot
Comm: Feria II after Lent III (gnpf., p.)

22 MARCH – TUESDAY – gnpf., p.
Feria III after Lent III

23 MARCH – WEDNESDAY – gnpf., p.
Feria IV after Lent III

+ LENTEN STATION AT THE
BASILICA OF SANTA MARIA ASSUNTA, AQUILEIA +

24 MARCH – THURSDAY – gd., w.
Saint Gabriel the Archangel
Comm: Feria V after Lent III (gnpf., p.)

25 MARCH – FRIDAY – d1, w./mb.

ANNUNCIATION OF THE BLESSED VIRGIN MARY AND COMMEMORATION OF OUR LADY OF WALSINGHAM

PATRONESS OF THE PONTIFICAL COURT
Comm: Feria VI after Lent III (gnpf., p.)

N.b. The Commemoration of O.L.W. may be simply the mass for the Annunciation, a separate mass said with the Common of the B.V.M., or the collect from the Common may be added as a commemoration to the Mass of the Annunciation.

26 MARCH – SATURDAY – gnpf., p.
Saturday after Lent III

✝ LENTEN STATION AT THE CATHEDRAL OF ST. DOMNIUS, SPLIT ✝

✚ 27 MARCH – SUNDAY – S1., sd., rs./p.

FOURTH SUNDAY IN LENT
ALSO KNOWN AS
LAETARE SUNDAY
Comm: Saint John of Damascus, C.D. (d., w.)

28 MARCH – MONDAY – sd., w.
Saint John Capistrano, Confessor
Comm: Feria II after Lent IV (gnpf., rs./p.)

29 MARCH – TUESDAY – gnpf., rs./p.
Feria III after Lent IV

30 MARCH – WEDNESDAY – gnpf., rs./p.
Feria IV after Lent IV

✝ LENTEN STATION AT THE CATHEDRAL OF ST. KILIAN, WÜRZBURG ✝

31 MARCH – THURSDAY – gnpf., rs./p.
Feria V after Lent IV

APRIL
LENT & PASCHALTIDE

1 APRIL – FRIDAY – gnpf., rs./p.
Feria VI after Lent IV

2 APRIL – SATURDAY – d., w.
Saint Francis de Paula, Confessor
Comm: Saturday after Lent IV (gnpf., p.)

+ LENTEN STATION AT THE CATHEDRAL OF ST. MARTIN, MAINZ +

*N.b. All crosses and images are either removed or veiled
in purple after None and prior to Vespers this day.*

*During Passiontide, the Gloria Patri is omitted
at all masses of the season.*

✚ 3 APRIL – SUNDAY – sı., sd., p.

PASSION SUNDAY

4 APRIL – MONDAY – d., w.
Saint Isidore
Bishop, Confessor, & Doctor of the Church
Comm: Feria II of Passion Week (gnpf., p.)

5 APRIL – TUESDAY – d., w.
Saint Vincent Ferrer, Confessor
Comm: Feria III of Passion Week (gnpf., p.)

6 APRIL – WEDNESDAY – gnpf., p.
Feria IV of Passion Week

+ LENTEN STATION AT THE CATHEDRAL OF ST. PETER, TRIER +

7 **APRIL** – **THURSDAY** – gnpf., p.
Feria V of Passion Week

8 **APRIL** – **FRIDAY** – gd., mb./w.
Our Lady of Seven Sorrows
Comm: Feria VI of Passion Week (gnpf., p.)

N.b. The Office may be of the feast or else of the feria with commemoration of the Seven Sorrows.

N.b. This feast is kept as a feast in the Anglican Patriarchate by tradition on Friday of Passion Week.

+ LENTEN STATION AT THE
SHRINE OF OUR LADY OF WALSINGHAM, NORFOLK +

9 **APRIL** – **SATURDAY** – gnpf., p.
Saturday of Passion Week

✚ 10 **APRIL** – **SUNDAY** – sı., sd., r.→p.

SECOND PASSION SUNDAY
OR
PALM SUNDAY

N.b. The Church is arrayed in purple paraments and then covered in red until after the procession, as appointed in the missal. If, however, the procession will not take place, the use of red is omitted.

N.b. During Holy Week prior to Good Friday, no feasts may be celebrated, but they may be commemorated until after the Feast of the Lord's Supper.

11 **APRIL** – **MONDAY** – gpf., p.

MONDAY OF HOLY WEEK

N.b. The Chrism Mass is said by the Bishop Ordinary on Monday or Tuesday of Holy Week. It does not take the place of the mass of the day. Instead, the mass of the day is said as usual in the morning, and this mass is said in the afternoon. However, the oils may alternatively be blessed on Holy Thursday morning, using the form appointed in the missal for the Chrism mass on that day.

N.b. The feast of Saint Leo I, P.C.D. (d., w.) is neither said nor commemorated this year.

12 APRIL – TUESDAY – gpf., p.

TUESDAY OF HOLY WEEK

13 APRIL – WEDNESDAY – gpf., p.

WEDNESDAY OF HOLY WEEK

N.b. The feast of Saint Hermenegild, M. (sd., r.) is neither said nor commemorated this year.

WITH THURSDAY OF HOLY WEEK BEGINS THE

Sanctum Triduum

INSTRUCTION IN THE EVENT THAT THE ENTIRE TRIDUUM CANNOT BE CELEBRATED

Taken from the Caeremoniale Aulae Sanctae Mariae Walsinghamensis:

The Sacred Triduum is one continuous liturgy. It either must be celebrated in its entirety or not at all. However, Good Friday is a Holy Day of Obligation. If the Triduum cannot be celebrated in its entirety, then:

    1) the mass of Holy Thursday is not said;

    2) the liturgy of Good Friday in the missal is said as given through the Veneration of the Cross inclusive, and there the liturgy ends;

3) the liturgy of Holy Saturday and the Easter Vigil are not said.

STRIPPING OF THE ALTAR ON HOLY THURSDAY IF THE TRIDUUM IS NOT CELEBRATED

If the full Triduum liturgy is not celebrated, the Offices naturally still take place, as said offices may be even private. Note that in the Mass of Holy Thursday, the altars are stripped before the Office of Vespers. Therefore, should the full liturgy not be performed, the altars are nevertheless stripped after None and before Vespers on the morning of Holy Thursday and remain thus until after None and before Vespers on the morning of Holy Saturday, being the first Office of Paschaltide.

14 APRIL – THURSDAY – dI, w.

FEAST OF THE LORD'S SUPPER

After the *Gloria in excelsis* of the Feast of the Lord's Supper, bells and musical instruments are not used again until the *Gloria* in the Mass of the Easter Vigil. A wooden instrument may be used in place of the bell when called for in the mass.

Both Vespers and Compline are said this day without chant. The altar is stripped after the mass, and the Sacrament is reserved at the Altar of Repose for the Mass of the Pre-Sanctified the following day in accordance with the rubrics. The Maundy is also performed after the mass as given in the rubrics in the missal.

N.b. If the Bishop expulsed public penitents on Ash Wednesday, then they are received in the Church again at a special mass this day in the manner prescribed in the Pontificale. The mass is a votive mass for the forgiveness of sins. If public penitents are to be received, then as a practical matter, the Chrism Mass should not be said on Maundy Thursday, but on Monday or Tuesday of Holy Week.

N.b. The feast of Saint Justin Martyr (d., r.) and Comm. of Sts. Tiburtius, Valerian, and Maximus, MM. (r.) is neither said nor commemorated this year.

15 APRIL – FRIDAY – gpf., b./p.

FRIDAY IN THE PASSION AND DEATH OF OUR LORD JESUS CHRIST
OTHERWISE KNOWN AS
GOOD FRIDAY

N.b. No mass is to be celebrated or commemorated this day other than the Mass of the Presanctified, and no elements are to be consecrated after the mass on Maundy Thursday until the Mass of the Easter Vigil exclusive. Vespers and Compline are again said this day without chant.

16 APRIL – SATURDAY – d1., p.→w.

HOLY SATURDAY AND EASTER VIGIL

N.b. Those who participate in the Holy Saturday and Easter Vigil rites fulfill their obligation to attend mass on Easter.

N.b. The rites of Holy Saturday and the vigil are held in the morning, following the norms for anticipated rites and offices of Lent and Passiontide. The Mass of Easter Vigil concludes with Solemn Vespers. The office of Compline is recited at its usual time in the evening, as throughout the year, and all offices return to the regular time.

✚ 17 APRIL – SUNDAY – s1, w.

SUNDAY IN THE RESURRECTION OF OUR LORD
OTHERWISE KNOWN AS
EASTER SUNDAY

N.b. The Feast of Saint Anicetus, P.M. (s., r.) is neither said nor commemorated this year according to the rubrics.

18 APRIL – MONDAY – octi, w.

EASTER MONDAY

19 APRIL – TUESDAY – octi, w.

EASTER TUESDAY

N.b. In general feasts may again be commemorated this day beginning at II Vespers, but no feasts may be celebrated until after Low Sunday.

20 APRIL – WEDNESDAY – octi, w.

WEDNESDAY OF EASTER WEEK

21 APRIL – THURSDAY – octi, w.

THURSDAY OF EASTER WEEK

Comm: Saint Anselm, B.C.D. (sd., w.)
– BIRTHDAY OF ROME –

22 APRIL – FRIDAY – octi, w.

FRIDAY OF EASTER WEEK

Comm: Saints Soter and Cajus, PP.MM. (sd., r.)

23 APRIL – SATURDAY – octi, w.

SATURDAY IN WHITE

Comm: Saint George, M. (sd., r.)

✤ 24 APRIL – SUNDAY – si., gd., w.

FIRST SUNDAY AFTER EASTER

OTHERWISE KNOWN AS

LOW SUNDAY

AND THE

COMMEMORATION OF THE DIVINE MERCY OF O.L.J.C.

Comm: Saint Fidelis of Sigmaringen, M. (sd., r.)

25 APRIL – MONDAY – d2, p.→w.

SAINT MARK, EVANGELIST
AND THE
GREATER LITANIES

Comm: Rogation Days as usual

✝ FESTAL STATION AT THE
BASILICA OF SANTA MARIA ASSUNTA, AQUILEIA ✝

N.b. The Procession of the Greater Litanies is held this day as usual.

26 APRIL – TUESDAY – sd., r.
Saints Cletus and Marcellinus, Popes & Martyrs

27 APRIL – WEDNESDAY – d., w.
Saint Peter Canisius, Confessor & Doctor

28 APRIL – THURSDAY – d., w.
Saint Paul of the Cross, Confessor
Comm: Saint Vitalis, M. (r.)

29 APRIL – FRIDAY – d., r.
Saint Peter of Verona, Martyr

30 APRIL – SATURDAY – d., w.
Saint Catherine of Sienna, Virgin

MAY

PASCHALTIDE & ASCENSION

✣ 1 MAY – SUNDAY – d2, r.

SAINTS PHILIP AND JAMES, APOSTLES
Comm: Easter II (sd., w.)

2 MAY – MONDAY – d., w.
Saint Athanasius
Bishop, Confessor, and Doctor of the Church

3 MAY – TUESDAY – d., r.
Invention of the Holy Cross
Comm: Saint Alexander I, P.M., Eventius and
Theodolus, MM, and Juvenalis, B.C. (r.)

N.b. On or around this day, crosses may be blessed to be
set in fields, vineyards, gardens, and other such
suitable locations as given in the Rituale.

4 MAY – WEDNESDAY – d., w.
Saint Monica, Widow

5 MAY – THURSDAY – d., w.
Saint Pius V, Pope and Confessor

6 MAY – FRIDAY – gd., r.
Saint John before the Lateran Gate

7 MAY – SATURDAY – d., r.
Saint Stanislas, Bishop and Martyr

✝ FESTAL STATION AT THE CATHEDRAL OF ST. DOMNIUS, SPLIT ✝

N.b. Also this day is the Feast of St. Domnius,
Bishop & Martyr

✚ **8 MAY – SUNDAY** – gd., w.
Apparition of Saint Michael
Comm: Easter III (sd., w.)

9 MAY – MONDAY – d., w.
Saint Gregory Nazianzen
Bishop, Confessor, & Doctor of the Church

10 MAY – TUESDAY – d., w.
Saint Antonius, Bishop & Confessor
Comm: Saints Gordian and Epimachus, MM. (r.)

N.b. Vespers of the Dead is said this day after
II Vespers of the feast.

11 MAY – WEDNESDAY – f., b.
Mass for the Dead on the First Ferial Day of May

N.b. The Office of the Dead is said this day. A second ferial
mass of the season may be said.

12 MAY – THURSDAY – sd., r.
Saints Nereus and Achilleus, Martyrs,
Saint Domitilla, V.M. and Saint Pacras, M.

13 MAY – FRIDAY – d., w.
Saint Robert Bellarmine
Bishop, Confessor, & Doctor of the Church

N.b. Vespers this day commemorates
the Saturday Office of Our Lady.

14 MAY – SATURDAY – s., mb./w.
Saturday Mass of Our Lady
Comm: Saint Boniface, M. (s., r.)

*N.b. The Office is the Saturday Office of Our
Lady through None.*

✚ 15 MAY – SUNDAY – d., w.
Saint John Baptist de la Salle, Confessor
Comm: Easter IV (sd., w.)

16 MAY – MONDAY – sd., w.
Saint Ubald, Bishop & Confessor

17 MAY – TUESDAY – d., w.
Saint Paschal Baylon, Confessor

18 MAY – WEDNESDAY – d., r.
Saint Venantius, Martyr

19 MAY – THURSDAY – d., w.
Saint Peter Celestine, Pope & Confessor

20 MAY – FRIDAY – sd., w.
Saint Bernardin of Siena, Confessor
Comm: St. Christopher Columbus, C. (sd., w.)

*N.b. Vespers this day commemorates
the Saturday Office of Our Lady.*

21 MAY – SATURDAY – s., mb./w.
Saturday Mass of Our Lady

*N.b. The Office is the Saturday Office of Our
Lady through None.*

13 FEBRUARY – SATURDAY – s., mb./w.
Saturday Mass of Our Lady

*N.b. The Office is the Saturday Office of Our
Lady through None.*

✠ 22 MAY – SUNDAY – sd., w.
Fifth Sunday after Easter

23 MAY – MONDAY – gnpf., p.
Rogation Monday and the Lesser Litanies

*N.b. The Procession of the Lesser Litanies is appointed for
the three Rogation Days. The local Ordinary, however, may
transfer these processions to another three consecutive days
according to the rubrics of the Liber Processionalis.*

24 MAY – TUESDAY – gnpf., p.
Rogation Tuesday and the Lesser Litanies

25 MAY – WEDNESDAY – maj. vig. 2, p.
VIGIL OF THE ASCENSION

*Comm: The Feasts of Saint Gregory VII, P.C. (d., w.) and
of Saint Urban I, P.M. (r.) and Rogation Wednesday and
the Lesser Litanies (gnpf., p.)*

---

*The Summer Half-Year begins this day
at First Vespers of the Ascension.*

✠ 26 MAY – THURSDAY – d1., w.

ASCENSION OF OUR LORD

Comm: Saint Philip Neri, C. (d., w.)

27 MAY – FRIDAY – d., w.
Saint Venerable Bede
Confessor & Doctor of the Church
Comm: Octave of the Ascension (oct., sd., w.)

28 MAY – SATURDAY – d2., gd., w.

SAINT AUGUSTINE OF CANTERBURY
BISHOP AND CONFESSOR
PATRON OF THE ANGLICAN RITE / ANGLO-ROMAN RITE
Comm: Octave of the Ascension (oct., sd., w.)

✠ 29 MAY – SUNDAY – oct., sd., w.

Sunday within the Octave of the Ascension
Comm: Saint Mary Magdalene of Pazzi, V. (sd., w.)

30 MAY – MONDAY – oct., sd., w.
Within the Octave of the Ascension
Comm: St. Felix I, P.M. (s., r.)

31 MAY – TUESDAY – d2, w./mb.

QUEENSHIP OF THE
BLESSED VIRGIN MARY

Comm: Octave of the Ascension (oct., sd., w.) and
St. Petronilla, V. (s., w.)

N.b. The office for this feast is of the B.V.M. with
commemoration of the Octave only according to the rubrics.

JUNE

ASCENSION, PENTECOST, & TRINITYTIDE

1 JUNE – WEDNESDAY – d2., gd., w.

SAINT AUGUSTINE OF CANTERBURY
BISHOP AND CONFESSOR
PATRON OF THE ANGLICAN RITE ROMAN CATHOLIC CHURCH
(TRANSFERRED)

Comm: Saint Angela Merici, V. (d., w.) and
Octave of the Ascension (oct., sd., w.)

2 JUNE – THURSDAY – oct., gd., w.
Octave Day of the Ascension
Comm: Saints Marcellinus and Peter, MM.
and Saint Erasmus, B.M. (s., r.)

3 JUNE – FRIDAY – f., w.
Feria VI after the Octave of the Ascension
N.b. The ferial mass this day is of the preceding Sunday
with modifications as given in the rubrics.

4 JUNE – SATURDAY – maj. vig. 1, p.→r.

SATURDAY IN
VIGIL OF THE PENTECOST
Comm: Saint Francis Caracciolo, C. (d., w.)
(only prior to the Vigil)

As during the Paschal Triduum, during the Triduum of
Whitsunday, feasts and votive masses may not be said, and
commemorations are not permitted. Commemorations are
again permitted beginning with Vespers on Whit Tuesday, but
feasts and votive masses may not be said throughout
Whitsunweek.

WITH THE SUNDAY OF PENTECOST BEGINS THE

Triduum de Pentecostes

✠ 5 JUNE – SUNDAY – SI., r.

WHITSUNDAY
ALSO KNOWN AS
PENTECOST

N.b. Saint Boniface, B.M. (d., r.) is neither said nor commemorated this year.

6 JUNE – MONDAY – dI., r.

WHIT MONDAY

N.b. Saint Norbert, B.C. (d., w.) is neither said nor commemorated this year.

7 JUNE – TUESDAY – dI., r.

WHIT TUESDAY

N.b. Commemorations may again be made as usual beginning at Vespers this day.

8 JUNE – WEDNESDAY – oct. I, sd., r.

EMBER WEDNESDAY OF WHITSUNWEEK

9 JUNE – THURSDAY – oct. 1, sd., r.

THURSDAY OF WHITSUNWEEK

Comm: Saints Primus and Felicianus, MM. (s., r.)

10 JUNE – FRIDAY – oct. 1, sd., r.

EMBER FRIDAY OF WHITSUNWEEK

Comm: Saint Margaret, Q.W. (sd., w.)

11 JUNE – SATURDAY – oct. 1, sd., r.

EMBER SATURDAY OF WHITSUNWEEK

Comm: Saint Barnabas, A. (gd., d2., r.)

WITH I VESPERS OF TRINITY SUNDAY BEGINS

Trinitytide

✚ 12 JUNE – SUNDAY – d1., w.

FEAST OF THE MOST HOLY TRINITY

*Comm: Saint John of Saint Facundo, C. (d., w.) and
Saints Cyrinus, Nabor, and Nazarius, MM. (r.)*

*N.b. Ferial masses until Thursday of this week exclusive
may be either of Trinity Sunday in white or of the
First Sunday after Pentecost in green.*

13 JUNE – MONDAY – d., w.

Saint Anthony of Padua,
Confessor & Doctor of the Church

N.b. It is as ancient custom to bless lilies on this day.

14 JUNE – TUESDAY – d., w.
Saint Basil the Great,
Bishop, Confessor, & Doctor of the Church

15 JUNE – WEDNESDAY – s., r.
Saints Vitus, Modestus, and Crescentia, Martyrs

✠ 16 JUNE – THURSDAY – dɪ. with oct. 2, w.

COMMEMORATION OF THE
MOST HOLY BODY AND BLOOD OF
OUR LORD JESUS CHRIST
ALSO KNOWN AS
THE FEAST OF CORPUS CHRISTI

PRINCIPAL FEAST DAY OF THE ORDER OF THE EAGLE OF
ST. STEPHEN AND MARY IMMACULATE

17 JUNE – FRIDAY – oct. 2, sd., w.
Within the Octave of Corpus Christi

18 JUNE – SATURDAY – oct. 2, sd., w.
Within the Octave of Corpus Christi
Comm: Saint Ephraem of Syria, Dc.C.D. (d., w.) and
Saints Mark and Marcellian, MM. (r.)

✠ 19 JUNE – SUNDAY – oct. 2, sd., w.
Sunday within the Octave of Corpus Christi
Comm: Saint Juliana of Falconieri, V. (d., w.) and Saints
Gervasius and Protasius, MM. (r.)

20 JUNE – MONDAY – oct. 2, sd., w.
Within the Octave of Corpus Christi
Comm: Saint Sylverius, P.M. (s., r.)

21 JUNE – TUESDAY – oct. 2, sd., w.
Within the Octave of Corpus Christi
Comm: Saint Aloysius Gonzaga, C. (d., w.)

22 JUNE – WEDNESDAY – oct. 2, sd., w.
Within the Octave of Corpus Christi
Comm: Saint Paulinus, B.C. (d., w.)

23 JUNE – THURSDAY – oct. 2, w.

OCTAVE DAY OF CORPUS CHRISTI

Comm: Vigil of the Nativity of
Saint John the Baptist (min. vig., p.)

24 JUNE – FRIDAY – s1. with oct. 3, w.

FEAST OF THE
SACRED HEART OF JESUS

**FEAST DAY OF THE ORDER OF THE EAGLE OF
ST. STEPHEN AND MARY IMMACULATE**

*N.b. The Feast of the Nativity of St. John the Baptist is
transferred to the following day due to the Feast of
the Sacred Heart.*

25 JUNE – SATURDAY – d1 with oct.3, w.

NATIVITY OF

SAINT JOHN THE BAPTIST
TRANSFERRED

Comm: Octave of the Sacred Heart (oct.3, w.)
and Saint William, A. (d., w.)

✠ **26 JUNE – SUNDAY** – d., r.

Saints John and Paul, Martyrs
Comm: Sunday within Octave of the Sacred Heart (oct.3, w.)
and Octave of Saint John Baptist (oct. 3, w.)

27 JUNE – MONDAY – oct.3, w.
Octave of the Sacred Heart
Comm: Octave of Saint John Baptist (oct. 3, w.)

28 JUNE – TUESDAY – d., r.
Saint Irenaeus, Bishop & Martyr
Comm: Octave of the Sacred Heart (oct.3, w.),
Octave of Saint John Baptist (oct. 3, w.), and Vigil of Saints
Peter and Paul, Apostles (min. vig., p.)

29 JUNE – WEDNESDAY – d1 with oct.3, r.

SAINTS PETER AND PAUL, APOSTLES
Comm: Octave of the Sacred Heart (oct.3, w.) and
Octave of Saint John Baptist (oct.3, w.)

✝ FESTAL STATION AT THE CATHEDRAL OF ST. PETER, TRIER ✝

30 JUNE – THURSDAY – gd., r.
Commemoration of Saint Paul, Apostle
Comm: Octave of the Sacred Heart (oct.3, w.) and
Octave of the Nativity of St. John Baptist (oct. 3, w.)

N.b.: In masses of the Commemoration of St. Paul the
Apostle, there is said the commemoration of Saint Peter
(as usual).

JULY

ഇഇരു

1 JULY – FRIDAY – gd., w.
Octave Day of the Sacred Heart
Comm: Octave Day of Saint John Baptist (gd., sd., w.) and
Octave of Saints Peter and Paul, AA. (oct. 3, r.)

N.b. The Precious Blood is transferred
to the following Sunday

◦◦◦◦◦

2 JULY – SATURDAY – d2, w./mb.
VISITATION OF THE
BLESSED VIRGIN MARY
Comm: Octave of Saints Peter & Paul, AA. (oct. 3, r.), and
Saints Processius & Martinian, MM (r.)

◦◦◦◦◦

✚ 3 JULY – SUNDAY – d1, r.

THE MOST PRECIOUS BLOOD OF
OUR LORD JESUS CHRIST
TRANSFERRED

Comm: Trinity III (sd., g.), Saint Leo II, P.C. (sd., w.), and
Octave of Saints Peter and Paul, AA. (oct. 3, r.)

◦◦◦◦◦

4 JULY – MONDAY – oct. 3, r.
Day VI within the Octave of
Saints Peter and Paul, Apostles

◦◦◦◦◦

5 JULY – TUESDAY – d., w.
Saint Anthony Maria Zacharias, Confessor
Comm: Octave of Saints Peter and Paul, AA. (oct. 3, r.)

◦◦◦◦◦

6 JULY – WEDNESDAY – gd., r.
Octave Day of Saints Peter and Paul, Apostles

◦◦◦◦◦

7 JULY – THURSDAY – d., w.
Saints Cyril and Methodius, Bishops and Confessors

8 JULY – FRIDAY – sd., w.
Saint Elizabeth of Portugal, Queen and Widow

✠ FESTAL STATION AT THE CATHEDRAL OF ST. KILIAN, WÜRZBURG ✠

*N.b. The Feast of St. Kilian, Apostle of Franconia,
is also celebrated or commemorated this day.*

*N.b. Vespers of the Dead is said after II Vespers of
the feast.*

9 JULY – SATURDAY – s., b.
Mass of the Dead on the First Ferial Day of July

*N.b. The Office of the Dead is said this day. A second ferial
mass may be said.*

✚ 10 JULY – SUNDAY – sd., g.
Fourth Sunday after Trinity
*Comm: Seven Holy Brothers, Martyrs, and Saints Rufina
and Secunda, Virgins and Martyrs (sd., r.)*

11 JULY – MONDAY – s., r.
Saint Pius I, Pope & Martyr

12 JULY – TUESDAY – d., w.
Saint John Gaulbert, Abbot
Comm: Saints Nabor and Felix, Martyrs (r.)

13 JULY – WEDNESDAY – sd., r.
Saint Anacletus, Pope and Martyr

14 JULY – THURSDAY – d., w.
Saint Bonaventure,
Bishop, Confessor, and Doctor of the Church

15 JULY – FRIDAY – sd., w.
Saint Henry, Emperor and Confessor

16 JULY – SATURDAY – gd., w./mb.
In Commemoration of Our Lady of Mount Carmel

✚ 17 JULY – SUNDAY – sd., g.
Fifth Sunday after Trinity
Comm: Saint Alexius, C. (sd., w.)

18 JULY – MONDAY – d., w.
Saint Camillus of Lellis, Confessor
Comm: Saint Symphorosa and Her Seven Sons, MM. (r.)

19 JULY – TUESDAY – d., w.
Saint Vincent de Paul, Confessor

20 JULY – WEDNESDAY – d., w.
Saint Jerome Emiliani, Confessor
Comm: Saint Margaret, V.M. (r.)

21 JULY – THURSDAY – s., w.
Saint Praxedes, Virgin

22 JULY – FRIDAY – d., w.
Saint Mary Magdalene, Penitent

23 JULY – SATURDAY – d., r.
Saint Apollinaris, Bishop & Martyr
Comm: Vigil of Saint James, Apostle (min. vig., p.) and
Saint Liborius, B.C. (w.)

✙ 24 JULY – SUNDAY – sd., g.
Sixth Sunday after Trinity
Comm: Saint Christina, V.M. (r.)

25 JULY – MONDAY – d2, r.

SAINT JAMES, APOSTLE

Comm: Saint Christopher, M. (r.)

26 JULY – TUESDAY – d2, w.

SAINT ANNE
MOTHER OF THE BLESSED VIRGIN MARY

27 JULY – WEDNESDAY – s., r.
Saint Pantaleon, Martyr

28 JULY – THURSDAY – sd., r.
Saints Nazarius and Celsus, MM., Saint
Victor I, P.M., and Saint Innocent I, P.C.

29 JULY – FRIDAY – sd., w.
Saint Martha, Virgin
Comm: Saints Felix II,
Simplicius, Faustinus, and Beatrice, MM. (r.)

N.b. Vespers this day commemorates
the Saturday Office of Our Lady.

47

30 JULY – SATURDAY – s., mb./w.
Saturday Mass of Our Lady
Comm: Saint Abdon and Sennem, Martyrs (s., r.)

N.b. The Office is the Saturday Office of Our Lady through None.

✚ **31 JULY – SUNDAY** – gd., d., w.
Saint Ignatius of Loyola, Confessor
Comm: Trinity VII (sd., g.)

AUGUST

TRINITYTIDE

1 AUGUST – MONDAY – gd., r.
Saint Peter's Chains
Comm: Saint Paul (as usual) and
of the Holy Maccabees, MM. (r.)

2 AUGUST – TUESDAY – d., w.
Saint Alfonse Maria de Liguori
Bishop, Confessor, and Doctor of the Church
Comm: Saint Stephen I, P.M. (r.)

3 AUGUST – WEDNESDAY – sd., r.
Invention of Saint Stephen, Deacon & Protomartyr
PATRON OF THE ANGLICAN PATRIARCHATE, STATO PONTIFICIO
ANGLICAN RITE ROMAN CATHOLIC CHURCH

+ FESTAL STATION AT THE
CATHEDRAL OF SANTA MARIA DEL FIORE, FLORENCE +

ALSO ANNUALLY THIS DAY:
FERRETRURIA,
…the principle temporal holiday of the Anglican Patriarchate, in
celebration of the heritage of the Etrurian / Tuscan territory,
Matilda, Margravine of Tuscany & Vice-Queen of Italy, and the
legacy of Pope Leo X as Cardinal Prince of Florence.

FEAST DAY OF THE ORDER OF THE EAGLE
OF ST. STEPHEN & MARY IMMACULATE

4 AUGUST – THURSDAY – gd., w.
Saint Dominic, Confessor

5 AUGUST – FRIDAY – gd., w./mb.
Dedication of Saint Mary of the Snows

6 AUGUST – SATURDAY – d2, w.
THE TRANSFIGURATION OF

Our Lord Jesus Christ

Comm: Saint Sixtus II, P.M., and
Saints Felicissimus and Agapitus, MM. (r.)

✠ 7 August – Sunday – d., w.

Saint Cajetan, Confessor

Comm: Trinity VIII (sd., g.) and Saint Donatus, B.M. (r.)

8 August – Monday – sd., r.

Saints Cyriacus, Largus, and Smaragdus, Martyrs

9 August – Tuesday – d., w.

Saint John Vianney, Confessor

Comm: Vigil of Saint Lawrence, M. (min. vig., p.) and
Saint Romanus, M. (r.)

10 August – Wednesday – d2 with oct., r.

Saint Lawrence, Martyr

N.b. As the Octave is simple, no mention is made of the
Octave in the Offices, except on the Octave Day, on
which it is commemorated in the Offices in Lauds and
II Vespers. For the Mass, the mass of the Octave yields to
feasts of simple rank and above, but not to those given
in the missal as commerorations.

11 August – Thursday – s., r.

Saint Tiburtius, Martyr, and
Saint Susanna, Virgin and Martyr

Comm: Octave of Saint Lawrence, M. (oct., r.)

12 August – Friday – d., w.

Saint Clare, Virgin

Comm: Octave of Saint Lawrence, M. (oct., r.)

13 AUGUST – SATURDAY – min. vig., p.
Vigil of the Assumption
of the Blessed Virgin Mary
Comm: Saints Hippolytus and Cassianus, MM. (r.) and
Octave of Saint Lawrence, M. (oct., r.)

N.b. The Offices are of the Vigil with Commemoration of the
Saints and without mention of the Octave.

✚ 14 AUGUST – SUNDAY – sd., g.
Ninth Sunday after Trinity
Comm: Saint Eusebius, Confessor (w.) and Octave of
Saint Lawrence, M. (oct., r.)

15 AUGUST – MONDAY – d1 with oct.3, w./mb.
ASSUMPTION OF THE
BLESSED VIRGIN MARY
Comm: Octave of Saint Lawrence, M. (oct., r.)

✝ FESTAL STATION AT THE
CATHEDRAL OF ST. STEPHEN AND SANTA MARIA ASSUNTA, PAVIA ✝

N.b. It is an ancient custom to bless herbs on this day.

ALSO ANNUALLY THIS DAY:
FERRAGOSTO

16 AUGUST – TUESDAY – d2, w.
SAINT JOACHIM
FATHER OF THE BLESSED VIRGIN MARY
CONFESSOR
Comm: Of the Octave of the Assumption of the B.V.M.
(oct. 3, w./mb.), and Of the Octave of
Saint Lawrence, M. (oct., r.)

ALSO ANNUALLY THIS DAY:
PALIO DELL'ASSUNTA

17 AUGUST – WEDNESDAY – d., w.
Saint Hyacinth, Confessor
Comm: Of the Octave of the Assumption of the B.V.M.
(oct. 3, w./mb.) and of the Octave Day
of Saint Lawrence, M. (oct. 3, r.)

18 AUGUST – THURSDAY – oct. 3, w./mb.
Of the Octave of the Assumption of the B.V.M.
Comm: Saint Agapitus, M. (r.)

19 AUGUST – FRIDAY – d., w.
Saint John Eudes, Confessor
Comm: Octave of the Assumption (oct. 3, w./mb.)

20 AUGUST – SATURDAY – d., w.
Saint Bernard
Abbot and Doctor of the Church
Comm: Octave of the Assumption of the B.V.M.
(oct. 3, w./mb.)

✚ 21 AUGUST – SUNDAY – d., w.
Saint Jane Frances Fremiot de Chantal, Widow
Comm: Trinity X (sd., g.) and the Octave of the Assumption
of the B.V.M. (oct. 3, w./mb.)

22 AUGUST – MONDAY – d2, w./mb.

THE IMMACULATE HEART OF THE
BLESSED VIRGIN MARY
OCTAVE DAY OF THE ASSUMPTION OF THE B.V.M.
Comm: Saints Tiburtius, Hippolytus,
and Symphorian, MM. (r.)

N.b. The Offices are of the BVM with commemoration of the
Octave Day and the martyrs.

23 AUGUST – TUESDAY – d., w.
Saint Philip Benizi, Confessor
Comm: Vigil of Saint Bartholomew, A. (min. vig., p.)

24 AUGUST – WEDNESDAY – d2, r.
SAINT BARTHOLOMEW, APOSTLE

25 AUGUST – THURSDAY – sd., d., w.
Saint Louis, King & Confessor

26 AUGUST – FRIDAY – s., r.
Saint Zephyrinus, Pope & Martyr

27 AUGUST – SATURDAY – sd., d., w.
Saint Joseph Calasanctius, Confessor

✚ 28 AUGUST – SUNDAY – d., w.
Saint Augustine
Bishop, Confessor, and Doctor of the Church
Comm: Trinity XI (sd., g.) and Saint Hermes, M. (sd., r.)

29 AUGUST – MONDAY – gd., w.
The Beheading of Saint John the Baptist
Comm: Saint Sabina, M. (r.)

30 AUGUST – TUESDAY – d., w.
Saint Rose of Lima, Virgin
Comm: Saints Felix and Adauctus, MM. (r.)

31 AUGUST – WEDNESDAY – d., w.
Saint Raymond Nonnatus, Confessor

SEPTEMBER

TRINITYTIDE

1 SEPTEMBER – THURSDAY – s., w.
Saint Giles, Abbot
Comm: Twelve Holy Brethren, MM. (r.)

2 SEPTEMBER – FRIDAY – sd., w.
Saint Stephen, King and Confessor

3 SEPTEMBER – SATURDAY – d., w.
Saint Pius X, Pope and Confessor

✚ **4 SEPTEMBER – SUNDAY** – sd., g.
Twelfth Sunday after Trinity

5 SEPTEMBER – MONDAY – sd., w.
Saint Lawrence Justinian, Bishop & Confessor

N.b. Vespers of the Dead is said after II Vespers of the Sunday.

6 SEPTEMBER – TUESDAY – s., b.
Mass of the Dead on the First Ferial Day of September

N.b. The Office of the Dead is said this day. A second ferial mass may be said.

7 SEPTEMBER – WEDNESDAY – f., g.
Feria IV after Trinity XII

8 SEPTEMBER – THURSDAY – d2, w./mb.
NATIVITY OF THE

BLESSED VIRGIN MARY
Comm: Saint Hadrian, M. (r.)

**+ FESTAL STATION AT THE
BASILICA OF SANTA MARIA ANTIQUA, ROME +**

*N.b. During the Octave, nothing is said in the Offices of the
Nativity of the B.V.M., including commemorations at Lauds
and Vespers, except during the Saturday Office (which is
not said this year) and on the Octave Day itself. However,
the Octave is commemorated at the Mass and is preferred
to feasts of simple rank.*

*And further note that it is an ancient custom to bless seeds
and seedlings on this day.*

9 SEPTEMBER – FRIDAY – oct., w./mb.
Of the Octave of the Nativity of the B.V.M.
Comm: Saint Gorgonius, M. (s., r.)

10 SEPTEMBER – SATURDAY – d., w.
Saint Nicholas of Tolentino, C.
Comm: Octave of the Nativity of the B.V.M. (oct., w./mb.)

✢ 11 SEPTEMBER – SUNDAY – sd., g.
Thirteenth Sunday after Trinity
*Comm: Octave of the Nativity of the B.V.M. (oct., w./mb.)
and Saint Protus and Hyacinth, MM. (s., r.)*

12 SEPTEMBER – MONDAY – gd., w./mb.
The Most Holy Name of Mary
Comm: Octave of the Nativity of the B.V.M. (oct., w./mb.)

13 SEPTEMBER – TUESDAY – oct., w./mb.
Octave of the Nativity of the B.V.M.

14 SEPTEMBER – WEDNESDAY – gd., r.
Exaltation of the Holy Cross
Comm: Octave of the Nativity of the B.V.M. (oct., w./mb.)

N.b. Vespers this day is of the following feast with commemoration of II Vespers of the Exaltation, and I Vespers of the Octave Day of the Nativity of the B.V.M.

15 SEPTEMBER – THURSDAY – d2., w./mb.

COMMEMORATION OF THE SEVEN SORROWS OF THE BLESSED VIRGIN MARY

Comm: Octave Day of the Nativity of the B.V.M. (s., w./mb.)

N.b. The Offices are said without commemoration of the Octave Day.

16 SEPTEMBER – FRIDAY – sd., r.
Saints Cornelius, Pope and Martyr, and Cyprian, Bishop and Martyr
Comm: Saints Euphemia, V., Lucy, and Geminian, MM. (r.)

17 SEPTEMBER – SATURDAY – d., w.
The Holy Stigmata of Saint Francis

✚ 18 SEPTEMBER – SUNDAY – d., w.
Saint Joseph of Cupertino, Confessor
Comm: Trinity XIV (sd., g.)

19 SEPTEMBER – MONDAY – d., r.
Saint Januarius, Bishop and Martyr, and His Companions

20 SEPTEMBER – TUESDAY – d., r.
Saint Eustace and Companions, Martyrs
Comm: Vigil of Saint Matthew, A.Ev. (min. vig., p.)

21 SEPTEMBER – WEDNESDAY – d2, r.

SAINT MATTHEW
APOSTLE AND EVANGELIST

Comm: Ember Wednesday in September (gnpf., p)

N.b. The Ember Days in September are the Wednesday, Friday, and Saturday of the Third Week in September, that is, the week beginning the Sunday in September that falls between the 12th and 18th inclusive.

22 SEPTEMBER – THURSDAY – d., w.
Saint Thomas of Villanova, Bishop and Confessor
Comm: Saint Maurice and Companions, MM. (r.)

23 SEPTEMBER – FRIDAY – sd., r.
Saint Linus, Pope & Martyr
Comm: Ember Friday in September (gnpf., p.)
and Saint Thecla, V.M. (r.)

24 SEPTEMBER – SATURDAY – gd., w./mb.
Our Lady of Ransom
Comm: Ember Saturday in September (gnpf., p.)

✙ **25 SEPTEMBER – SUNDAY** – sd., g.
Fifteenth Sunday after Trinity

26 SEPTEMBER – MONDAY – s., r.
Saints Cyprian and Justina, Martyrs

27 SEPTEMBER – TUESDAY – sd., r.
Saint Cosmas and Damian, Martyrs

28 SEPTEMBER – WEDNESDAY – sd., r.
Saint Wencelas, Duke and Martyr

29 SEPTEMBER – THURSDAY – d1, w.

SAINT MICHAEL AND ALL ANGELS

30 SEPTEMBER – FRIDAY – d., w.
*Saint Jerome
Priest, Confessor, and Doctor of the Church*

*N.b. Vespers this day commemorates
the Saturday Office of Our Lady.*

OCTOBER

TRINITYTIDE

ରେଓଓ

1 OCTOBER – SATURDAY – s., mb./w.
Saturday Mass of Our Lady
Comm: Saint Remigius, B.C. (s., w.)

N.b. The Office is the Saturday Office of Our Lady through None.

⬩⬩⬩

✚ 2 OCTOBER – SUNDAY – gd., w.
The Holy Guardian Angels
Comm: Trinity XVI (sd., g.)

⬩⬩⬩

3 OCTOBER – MONDAY – d., w.
Saint Teresa of the Child Jesus, Virgin

⬩⬩⬩

4 OCTOBER – TUESDAY – gd., w.
Saint Francis of Assisi, Confessor

⬩⬩⬩

5 OCTOBER – WEDNESDAY – s., r.
Saint Placidus and Companions, Martyrs

⬩⬩⬩

6 OCTOBER – THURSDAY – d., w.
Saint Bruno, Abbot

⬩⬩⬩

7 OCTOBER – FRIDAY – d2, w./mb.

COMMEMORATION OF
OUR LADY OF VICTORY

ALSO KNOWN AS

THE HOLY ROSARY
OF THE BLESSED VIRGIN MARY

Comm: Saint Mark, P.C. (s., w.), and Saints Sergius, Bacchus, Marcellus, and Apulejus, Martyrs (s., r.)

8 OCTOBER – SATURDAY –d., w.
Saint Bridget of Sweden, Widow

✚ **9 OCTOBER** – SUNDAY – d., w.
Saint John Leonard
Comm: St. Pius XII, P.C. (sd., w.), Trinity XVII (sd., g.) and Saint Denys, Bishop and Martyr, and Rusticus and Eleutherius, Martyrs (sd., r.)

N.b. The mass for St. Pius XII is Si Diliges Me for Popes.

10 OCTOBER – MONDAY – sd., w.
Saint Francis Borgia, Confessor

11 OCTOBER – TUESDAY – d2, w./mb.

MOTHERHOOD OF THE BLESSED VIRGIN MARY

N.b. Vespers of the Dead is said this day after II Vespers of the feast.

12 OCTOBER – WEDNESDAY – f., b.
Mass for the Dead on the First Ferial Day of October

N.b. The Office of the Dead is said this day. A second ferial mass of the season may be said.

13 OCTOBER – THURSDAY – sd., w.
Saint Edward, King and Confessor

14 OCTOBER – FRIDAY – d., r.
Saint Callistus, Pope and Martyr

15 OCTOBER – SATURDAY – d., w.
Saint Teresa, Virgin

✤ 16 OCTOBER – SUNDAY – sd., g.
Eighteenth Sunday after Trinity
Comm: Saint Hedwig, W. (sd., w.)

17 OCTOBER – MONDAY – d., w.
Saint Margaret Mary Alacoque, Virgin

18 OCTOBER – TUESDAY – d2, r.
SAINT LUKE THE EVANGELIST

19 OCTOBER – WEDNESDAY – d., w.
Saint Peter of Alcantara, Confessor

20 OCTOBER – THURSDAY – d., w.
Saint John Cantius, Confessor

21 OCTOBER – FRIDAY – s., w.
Saint Hilarion, Abbot
Comm: Saints Ursula and Companions, MM (r.)

*N.b. Vespers this day commemorates
the Saturday Office of Our Lady.*

22 OCTOBER – SATURDAY – s., mb./w.
Saturday Mass of Our Lady

*N.b. The Office is the Saturday Office of Our
Lady through None*

✚ 23 October – Sunday – sd., g.
Nineteenth Sunday after Trinity

24 October – Monday – gd., w.
Saint Raphael the Archangel

25 October – Tuesday – s., r.
Saints Chrysanthus and Daria, Martyrs

26 October – Wednesday – s., r.
Saint Evaristus, Pope & Martyr

27 October – Thursday – min. vig., p.
Vigil of Saints Simon and Jude, Apostles

28 October – Friday – d2, w.

Saints Simon and Jude, Apostles

*N.b. Vespers this day commemorates
the Saturday Office of Our Lady.*

29 October – Saturday – s., mb./w.
Saturday Mass of Our Lady

*N.b. The Office is the Saturday Office of Our
Lady through None*

✚ 30 October – Sunday – d2, r.

The Kingship of
Our Lord Jesus Christ
Comm: Trinity XX (sd., g.)

*N.b. As the Feast of Christ the King is always kept
on the last Sunday of October. And further note that*

Vespers this day is, this year, instead of the Feast of All Saints with commemoration of the Kingship as usual.

31 OCTOBER – MONDAY – min. vig., p.
Vigil of All Saints

N.b. The Office begins with Matins and ends with None.

NOVEMBER

TRINITYTIDE

✚ 1 NOVEMBER – TUESDAY – d1, w.

FEAST OF ALL SAINTS

✝ FESTAL STATION AT THE BASILICA OF ST. PETER, ROME ✝

N.b. Vespers of All Saints is said as usual. Then follows immediately Vespers and Compline in Commemoration of All the Faithful Departed.

2 NOVEMBER – WEDNESDAY – d., b.

Commemoration of All the Faithful Departed
otherwise known as All Souls' Day
Comm: Octave of All Saints (oct. 3, w.)

N.b. Matins is said only of the dead this day, with commemoration of the Octave at Lauds. The Office for All Souls' Day ends with None. Vespers is of the following.

3 NOVEMBER – THURSDAY – oct. 3, w.
Of the Octave of All Saints

4 NOVEMBER – FRIDAY – d., w.
Saint Charles Borromeo, Bishop and Confessor
Comm: Fourth Day in the Octave of All Saints (oct. 3, w.), and Saints Vitalis and Agricola, MM. (r.)

5 NOVEMBER – SATURDAY – oct. 3, w.
Fifth Day in the Octave of All Saints

✠ 6 NOVEMBER – SUNDAY – sd., g.

Twenty-First Sunday after Trinity

Comm: Sixth Day in the Octave of All Saints (oct. 3, w.),

7 NOVEMBER – MONDAY – d., w.

SAINT WILLIBRORD

FIRST BISHOP OF UTRECHT

Comm: Seventh Day in the Octave of All Saints (oct. 3, w.)

N.b. The mass of the saint is Missa Statuit, the first mass from the Common of Confessor Bishops in the missal.

8 NOVEMBER – TUESDAY – gd., w.

Octave Day of All Saints

Comm: Four Crowned Martyrs (r.)

9 NOVEMBER – WEDNESDAY – d2, w.

DEDICATION OF THE ARCHBASILICA OF OUR SAVIOUR

Comm: Saint Theodore, M. (r.)

10 NOVEMBER – THURSDAY – d., w.

Saint Andrew Avellino, Confessor

*Comm: Saints Tryphon, Respicius, MM.,
and Nympha, V.M. (r.)*

11 NOVEMBER – FRIDAY – d., w.

Saint Martin, Bishop and Confessor

Comm: Saint Mennas, M. (r.)

✠ FESTAL STATION AT THE
CATHEDRAL OF ST. MARTIN DE TOURS, MAINZ ✠

12 NOVEMBER – SATURDAY – sd., r.

Saint Martin I, Pope & Martyr

✙ 13 NOVEMBER – SUNDAY – sd., g.
Twenty-Second Sunday after Trinity
Comm: Saint Didacus, C. (sd., w.)

14 NOVEMBER – MONDAY – d., r.
Saint Josephat, Bishop and Martyr

15 NOVEMBER – TUESDAY – d., w.
Saint Albert the Great
Bishop, Confessor, and Doctor of the Church

16 NOVEMBER – WEDNESDAY – d., w.
Saint Gertrude, Virgin

17 NOVEMBER – THURSDAY – sd., w.
Saint Gregory the Wonderworker, Bishop & Confessor

18 NOVEMBER – FRIDAY – gd., w.
Dedication of the Basilicas
of the Holy Apostles Peter and Paul
Comm: Trinity XXIII (sd., g.) transferred

N.b. The Trinity XXIII mass, if celebrated, has
all the privileges of a Sunday.

19 NOVEMBER – SATURDAY – d., w.
Saint Elizabeth of Hungary, Widow
Comm: Trinity XXIV (sd., g.) transferred,
and Saint Pontianus, P.M. (r.)

N.b. The Trinity XXIV mass, if celebrated, has
all the privileges of a Sunday.

✝ 20 NOVEMBER – SUNDAY – d., w.
Saint Felix de Valois, Confessor
Comm: Sunday Next before Advent (sd., g.)

21 NOVEMBER – MONDAY – gd., w./mb.
Presentation of the Blessed Virgin Mary

22 NOVEMBER – TUESDAY – d., r.
Saint Cecilia, Virgin and Martyr

23 NOVEMBER – WEDNESDAY – d., r.
Saint Clement I, Pope and Martyr
Comm: Saint Felicitas, M. (r.)

24 NOVEMBER – THURSDAY – d., w.
Saint John of the Cross
Confessor and Doctor of the Church
Comm: Saint Chrysogonus, M. (r.)

---

*The Winter Half–Year begins this day
at First Vespers of Saint Catherine.*

---

25 NOVEMBER – FRIDAY – d., r.
Saint Catherine, Virgin and Martyr

26 NOVEMBER – SATURDAY – d., w.
Saint Sylvester, Abbot
Comm: Saint Peter of Alexandria, B.M. (r.)

✚ **27 NOVEMBER – SUNDAY** – d₁, sd., p.

FIRST SUNDAY IN ADVENT

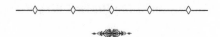

28 NOVEMBER – MONDAY – gnpf., p.
Feria II after Advent I

29 NOVEMBER – TUESDAY – min. vig., p.
Vigil of Saint Andrew the Apostle
Comm: Saint Saturninus, M. (r.)

30 NOVEMBER – WEDNESDAY – d₁, r.

SAINT ANDREW THE APOSTLE